AMIGURUMI FA AND FOREST FRIENDS

26 Cute Crochet Creations

Rosa O Collier

Table of Contents

Introduction

Welcome to *Amigurumi Farm and Forest Friends: 26 Cute Crochet Creations!* This book will show you how to make adorable stuffed animal projects in the popular Japanese style of amigurumi, with bright colors and big, exaggerated features.

Fun for beginners and experts alike, these projects require very little material and take only a couple hours. In the following pages you'll get an introduction to the essential terminology and techniques you'll need to crochet them. Then it's on to twenty-six animal patterns developed by talented craft artists from all over the world, complete with full-color photographs to help you follow along.

Step-by-step instructions will teach you how to make a spotted cow, a curly-tailed pig, a prickly porcupine, and much, much more.

Happy hooking!

Notes on Tools and Materials

Yarn

I prefer to use acrylics for amigurumi (the Japanese word, now used worldwide, for knitted or crocheted stuffed figures), because they are easily available, come in a wide range of colors, and they work up into sturdy, machine-washable pieces.

The patterns in this book were designed with DK (light worsted) yarn, but you could use any yarn thickness: as long as you stick to it throughout, your dolls will turn out fine, just slightly smaller or bigger than the original.

Stitch Markers

These are sometimes necessary to mark specific stitches for orientation later. Also, because most amigurumi is worked in a continuous spiral without joining, you will need a stitch marker to keep track of your rounds. There are special split-ring markers for crochet, but safety pins or paper clips work just as well.

Stuffing

I recommend polyester fiberfill, as it is easily available and economical, and makes resilient, washable toys. Stuffing settles over time, so (unless instructed otherwise) stuff pieces firmly so they will maintain their appearance for a long time.

A pair of tweezers will come in handy when you need to stuff narrow pieces or fill parts through small openings.

Needles and Pins

Blunt tapestry needles are usually recommended for sewing knit and crochet pieces, but for amigurumi, I prefer a chenille needle (large embroidery needle) because its sharp point can pierce through yarn if necessary for a neat join. Though not an absolute necessity, a small embroidery needle gives you better control when creating fine details like a mouth.

Craft pins are used to hold pieces in place while you sew them together.

Plastic Eyes

The eye sizes in this book are applicable for DK yarn; if you use a different yarn thickness, you will need to adjust the eye size accordingly. The instructions for eye placement always refer to the distance between the eye shafts/center of the eyes, which remains constant regardless of yarn weight and eye size. For perfectly placed eyes, stuff the head, and then use pins to find the right position. Stick the eyes in place, then remove the stuffing so you can attach the washers (washers should be pushed onto the eye stems with the bulge pointing away from the eye).

Please note that small plastic parts should always be considered a choking hazard for babies, so even safety eyes should be avoided. If making dolls for a young recipient, use embroidery to create the eyes.

Hook size: At the beginning of each pattern, a desired hook size is listed. Hook sizes range, from small at the beginning of the alphabet (nothing in this book is smaller than a C/2) to larger as the letters go on. The hook size affects the gauge, the number of stitches in a square inch, and the finished project size. Tighter stitches will ensure that stuffing won't emerge through gaps, although they should be loose enough to work through them with the hook.

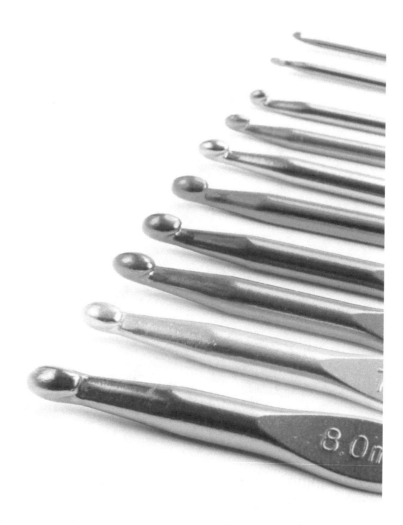

Reading a pattern: The patterns in this book are mostly in rounds (Rnd), meaning instead of being made in flat "rows" of stitches, they're worked in circular rows of stitches, or "rounds." Some crochet makers use a stitch marker to keep track of the start of each round. Asterisks surrounding instructions indicate to repeat that set of steps.

A number within parentheses at the end of each step indicates how many stitches should be in that round, when complete, not counting chain stitches.

Example: *1sc, sc2tog, 1sc* (12)
Translation: Single crochet in the first stitch, decrease over the next two stitches, and then single crochet in the next stitch. Repeat this process until the round is finished, giving you 12 stitches in that round.

Parentheses inside asterisks are separate steps that need to be repeated in addition to repeating the entire asterisked set. In this book, an "x" should be read as "times."

Example: *2sc in next stitch, (1sc) 4x* (12)
Translation: Single crochet twice in the next stitch, then single crochet into the next four stitches, and repeat.

Crochet Techniques

Before you start any of the twenty-six cute patterns in this book, practice the various stitches and learn their abbreviations.

Slip Knot: Every crochet project begins with a slip knot.
  1. Wrap the yarn around your finger, creating a loop with a 6" tail. **(fig. a)**

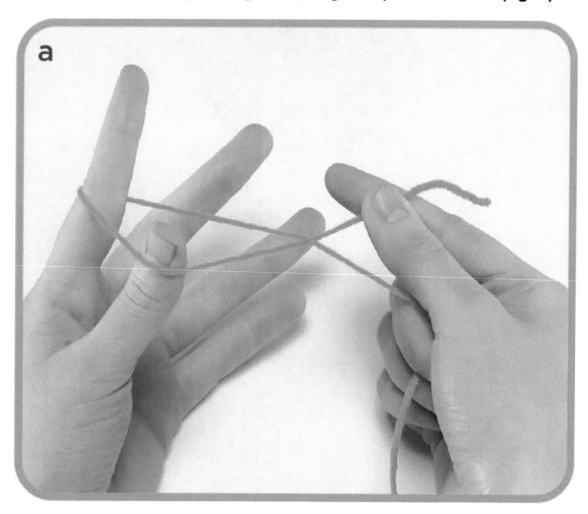

2. Pull one end of the yarn through the loop to create a knot. The knot should be taut, but not too tight to slip your hook through. **(figs. b and c)**

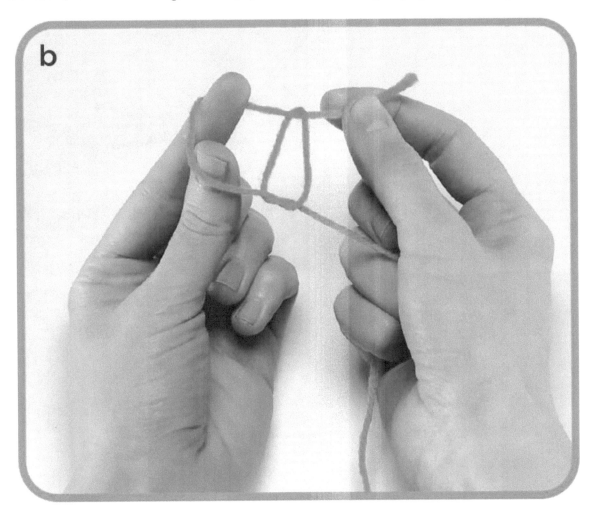

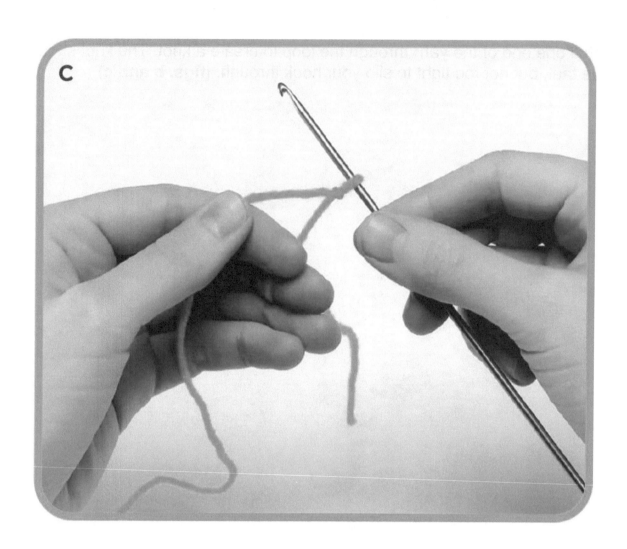

Yarn Over (yo): A basic technique that's used frequently, "yarn over" simply means to wrap the yarn over the hook.

1. With your hook in your right hand and your yarn in your left, pull the yarn around from behind the hook.
2. The strand of your "working yarn" (the yarn coming from the skein) should be across the throat of your hook on top. **(fig. d)**

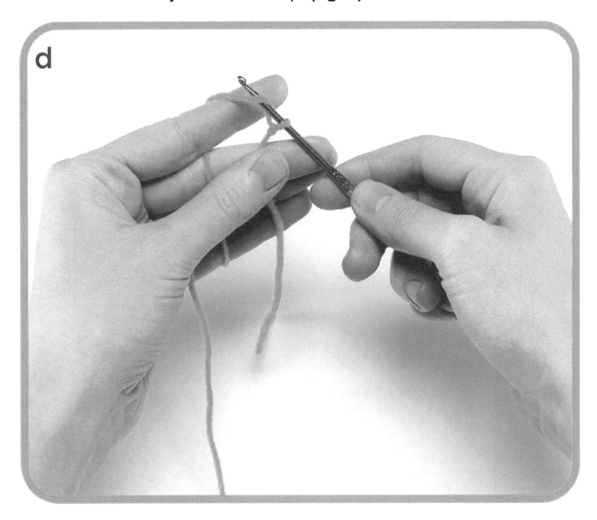

Chain Stitch (ch): The most basic crochet stitch, the chain stitch, forms the foundation row or ring for every crochet project. For most of the projects in this book, you will be working in a ring.

 1. To begin a chain stitch, start with a slip knot. **(fig. c)**
 2. Yo, then draw yarn through the loop, making the first stitch. Continue working in this manner until you have the desired number of stitches. **(fig. d and e)**

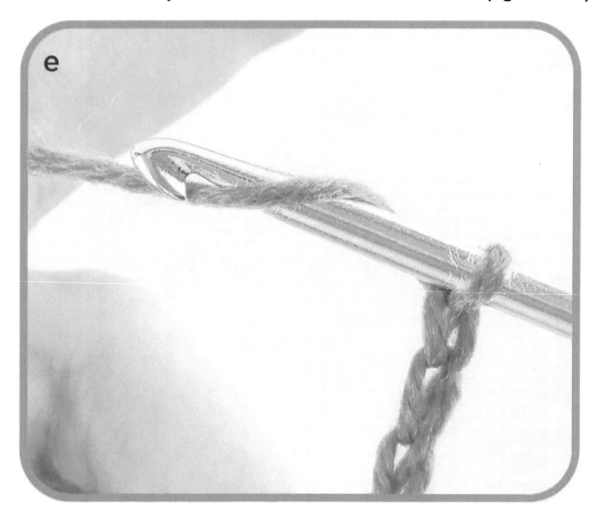

Working into the chain: Occasionally a pattern will say to work into the front or back of a chain. The front of the chain looks like a series of V's, and the back of the chain has a ridge (or bump) behind each chain stitch. **(fig. f)**

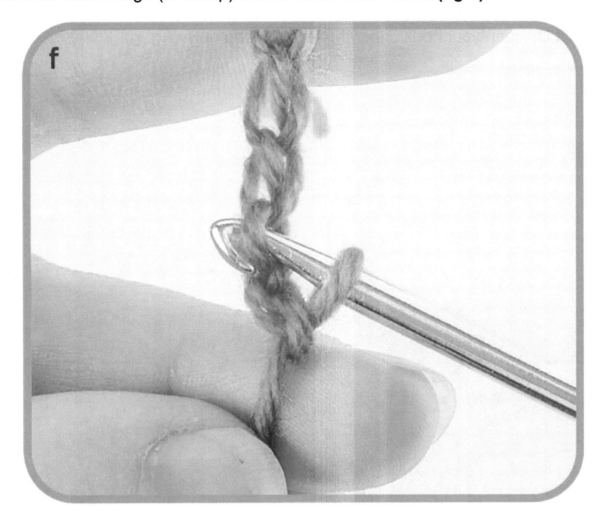

Working in Front/Back Loop Only (FLO/BLO):

When you look at the V on top of the stitch, the strand closest to you is called the front loop and the strand farthest from you is called the back loop. If you need to work in FLO, insert your hook under the closest loop only. If you need to work BLO, insert your hook under the farthest loop only. **(fig. g)**

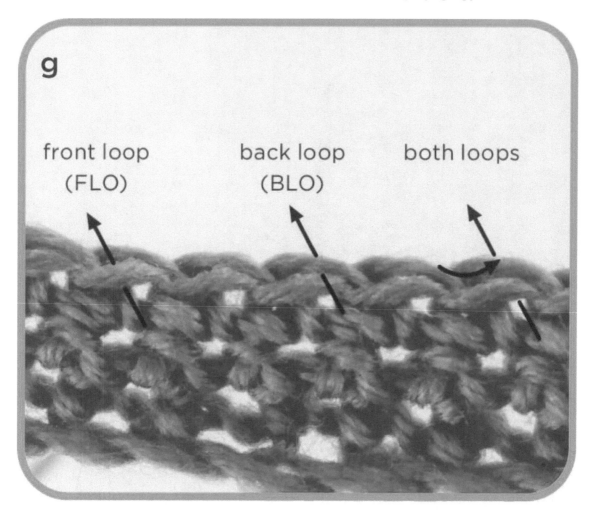

g

front loop (FLO)   back loop (BLO)   both loops

Single Crochet (sc):

1. Insert hook into desired stitch. **(fig. h)**

2. Yo and draw yarn through loop. You will now have two loops on your hook. **(figs. i and j)**

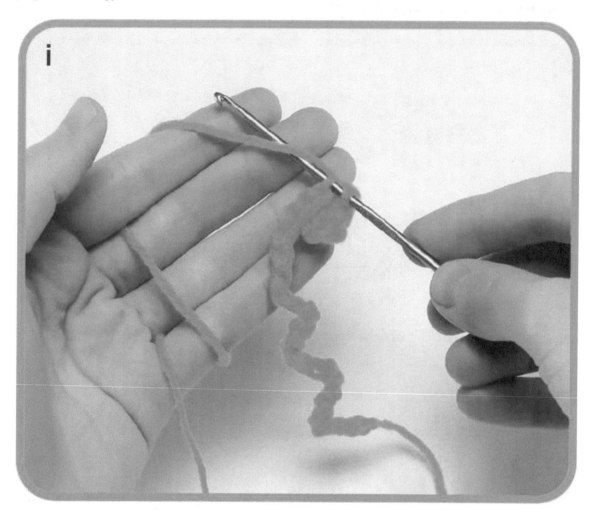

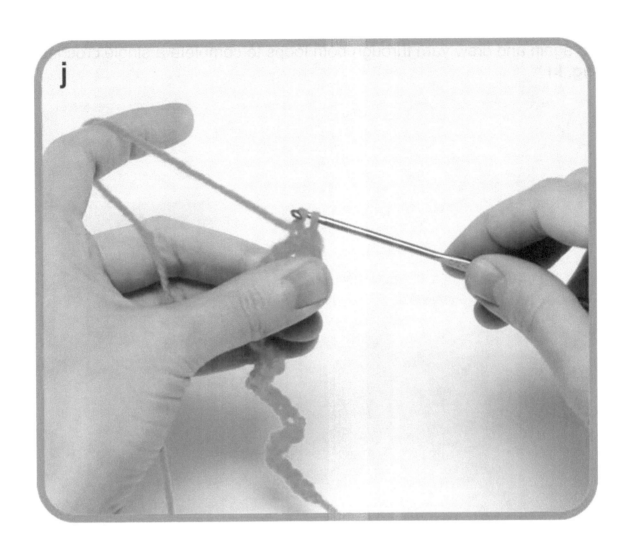

j

3. Yo again and draw yarn through both loops to complete a single crochet. **(fig. k)**

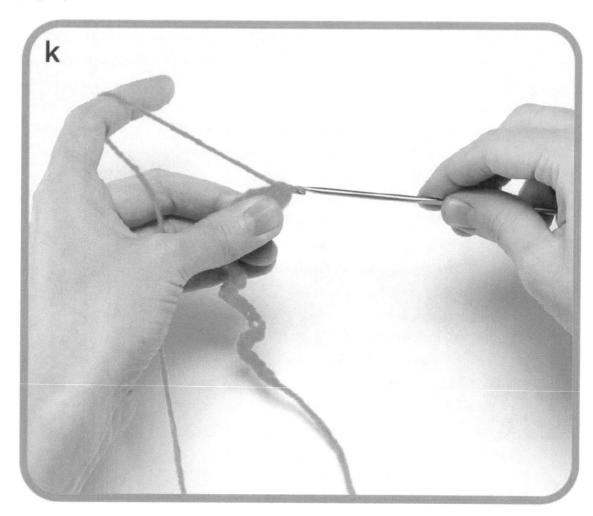

k

Half Double Crochet (hdc): This stitch is between single crochet and double crochet in height.
1. Yo and insert the hook into the desired stitch.
2. Yo and draw yarn through the stitch, leaving three loops on your hook.
3. Yo one last time and draw yarn through all three loops.

Slip Stitch (sl st): This stitch is used to connect pieces, strengthen edges, or fasten off stitches.
1. Insert your hook into the st or ch
2. YO, and pull yarn through both the st or ch and the loop on hook. **(fig. I)**

Be careful to keep the stitch loose: the V on top should be the same size as the top of other stitches. If your sl st is too tight, you won't be able to insert your hook in the next round, or your work might pucker.

Double Crochet (dc): The double crochet, the most commonly used stitch, is about as tall as two rows of single crochet.

1. Yo, then insert hook into a desired stitch. **(fig. m)**

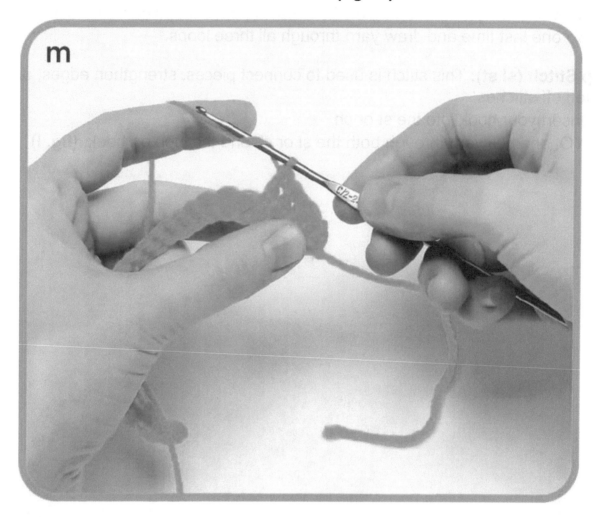

2. Yo, then draw your hook through the stitch, leaving three loops on the hook. **(fig. n)**

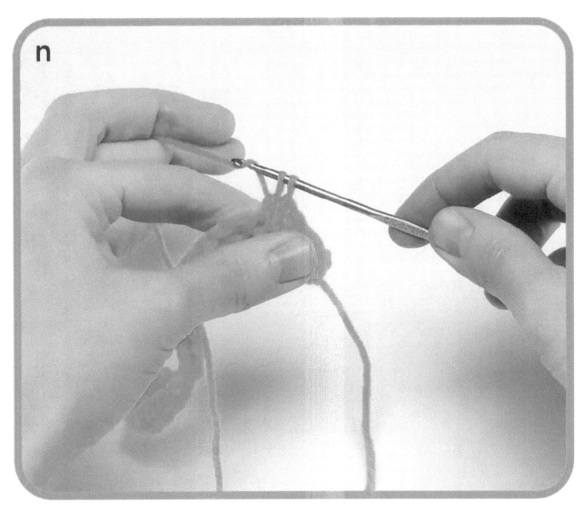

3. Yo, then draw yarn through first two loops on the hook, leaving two loops on hook.

4. Yo one more time and pull yarn through last two remaining loops. **(fig. o)**

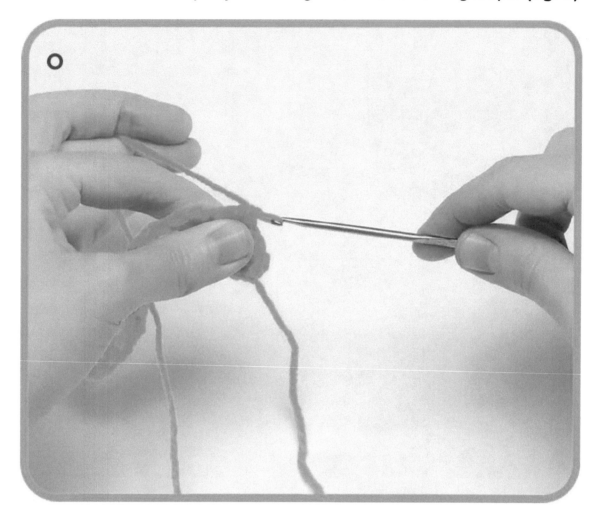

Treble Crochet (tr): This stitch is used to make the tallest stitches.

1. Yo two times, then insert hook into desired stitch.

2. Yo and draw yarn through stitch, leaving you with four loops on the hook.

3. Yo and draw yarn through the first two loops, leaving three loops on the hook.

4. Yo and draw yarn through two loops, leaving two loops on the hook.

5. Yo again, and draw yarn through the last two loops, leaving just one loop.

Decreasing (sc2tog): This abbreviation for decreasing means to single crochet the next two stitches together. By doing this, you will combine stitches, making the piece smaller.

1. Insert hook in desired stitch, yo and draw yarn through stitch.
2. Insert hook in the next stitch, yo and draw yarn through, leaving three loops on the hook. **(fig. p)**

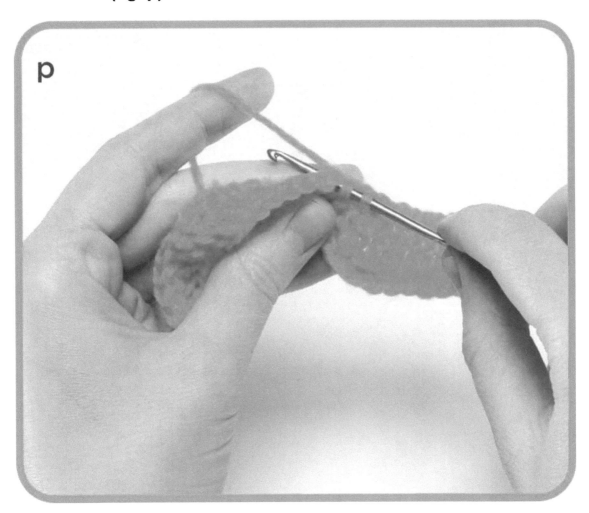

3. Yo, then draw yarn through all three loops. **(figs. q and r)**

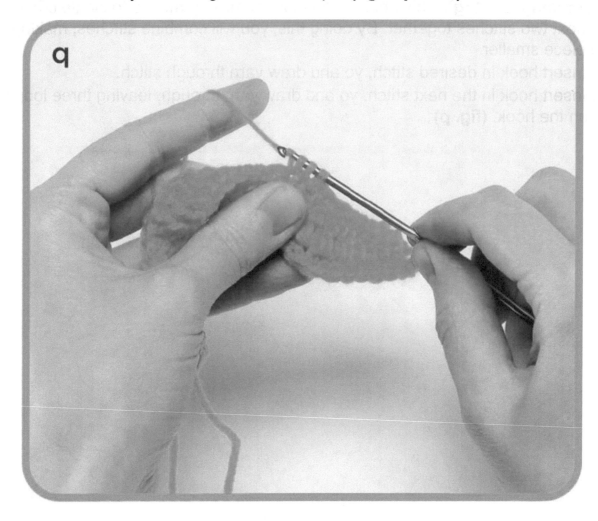

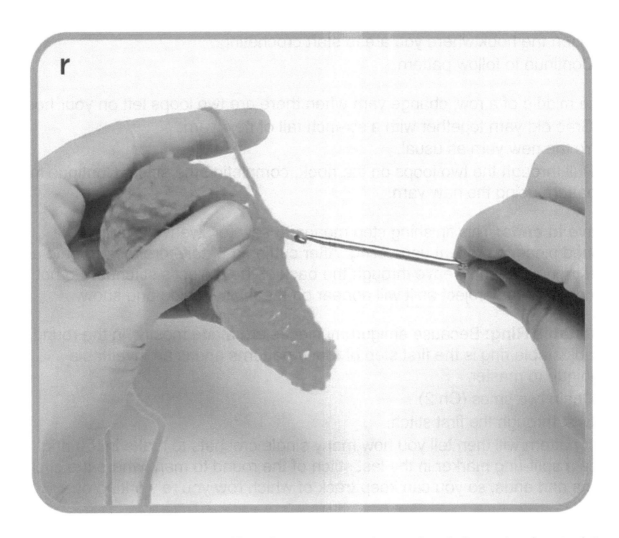

Front Post Double Crochet (fpdc): Yarn over, insert hook from the front of the post, going into the back, then coming out to the front again, draw up a loop, yarn over, pull through two loops, yarn over and pull through both loops.

Back Post Double Crochet (bpdc): Yarn over, insert hook from the back of the post, going into the front, then coming out to the back again, draw up a loop, yarn over and pull through two loops, yarn over and pull through both loops.

Invisible Decrease (invdec): Insert your hook in the front loop only of the st (no yo). Swing the hook slightly downward so you can insert it into the front loop of the next st. Yo and draw up a loop through both front loops. Yo and pull through the 2 loops on hook.

Adding yarn: To change colors or start on a new skein after running out of yarn, follow these simple steps.

At the end of a row:
   1. Make a slip knot with the new skein, leaving a tail.

2. Insert the hook where you are to start crocheting.

3. Continue to follow pattern.

In the middle of a row, change yarn when there are two loops left on your hook:

1. Grab old yarn together with a six-inch tail of new yarn.

2. Yo the new yarn as usual.

3. Pull through the two loops on the hook, completing the stitch. Continue in pattern using the new yarn.

Weave in ends: This finishing step means to sew (or "weave") yarn into a finished piece to prevent unraveling. After cutting a 6" tail, thread yarn onto a tapestry needle and weave through the back of the project's stitches. Do not go in and out of the project as it will appear on the finished side and show.

Adjustable Ring: Because amigurumi pieces are made mostly "in the round," the adjustable ring is the first step of many patterns and is an invaluable technique to master.

1. Chain two times (Ch 2).

2. Sl st through the first stitch.

Each pattern will then tell you how many single crochets to make in the ring. Place a split-ring marker in the last stitch of the round to mark where the circle begins and ends, so you can keep track of which row you're working on.

Abbreviation Chart

Abbreviation	Term
ch	chain
sc	single crochet
sl st	slip stitch
st	stitch
hdc	half double crochet
Invdec	Invisible decrease
dc	double crochet
tr	treble crochet
sc2tog	single crochet 2 together
rnd(s)	round(s)
rows	no abbreviation
yo	yarn over
TBL	through back loop
BLO	back loop only
TFL	through front loop
FLO	front loop only
fbdc	front post double crochet
bpdc	back post double crochet

monkey

FROM KARLA FITCH IN CLEVELAND, OHIO

Karla Fitch began designing toys while transitioning from working at a Fortune 500 company to being a stay-at-home mom. She couldn't stop being creative, and we are so glad! After you finish this adorable monkey, you might be the one swinging from tree to tree! But don't turn your back on this guy, as he is one sneaky little monkey!

what you'll need:

- F/5 (3.75 mm) crochet hook
- worsted weight cotton yarn in dark brown and tan
- black safety eyes (9 mm)
- black embroidery floss
- chenille needle
- embroidery needle
- stuffing

FINISHED SIZE: About 10 inches tall

Instructions

MOUTH: Tan yarn
- Ch9

Rnd 1: 2sc in 2nd ch from hook. (1sc) 6x, 4sc in last st. Rotate piece 180 degrees to the right to work along the opposite side of the chain. (1sc) 6x, 2sc in last st (20). **(fig. 1a)**

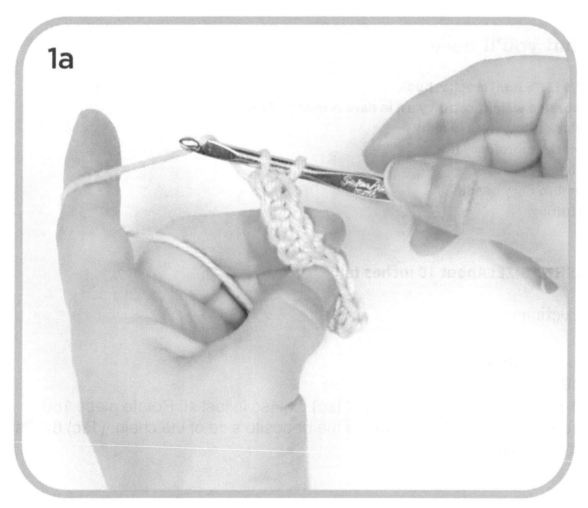

Rnd 2: 1sc in each st (20)

Rnd 3: 1sc in each st (20)

• Join with sl st to first stitch in Rnd 3 and finish off, leaving a tail for sewing.

• Use black embroidery floss to stitch mouth and nostrils. **(fig. 1b)**

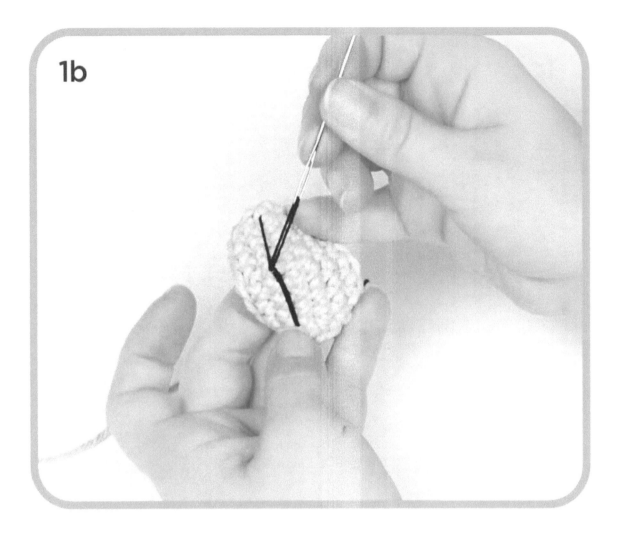

EARS (MAKE 2): Tan yarn
• Make adjustable ring.
Rnd 1: 6sc in ring (6)
Rnd 2: 2sc in each st (12)
Rnd 3: *2sc in next st, 1sc* (18)
Rnd 4: *sc2tog, 1sc* (12)
• Finish off, leaving a tail for sewing.

EYES (MAKE 2): Tan yarn
• Ch4
Working in rows:
Row 1: 1sc in 2nd ch from hook. 1sc in each st (3). Ch1 and turn.
Row 2: 1sc in each st (3). Ch1 and turn.
Row 3: (1sc) 2x, (2sc in next st) 1x. Rotate piece 90 degrees—so the left edge faces up. 1hdc in the middle of the rows. Rotate piece 90 degrees again—so the bottom edge faces up. (2sc in next st) 1x, (1sc) 1x. (9) **(fig. 1c)**

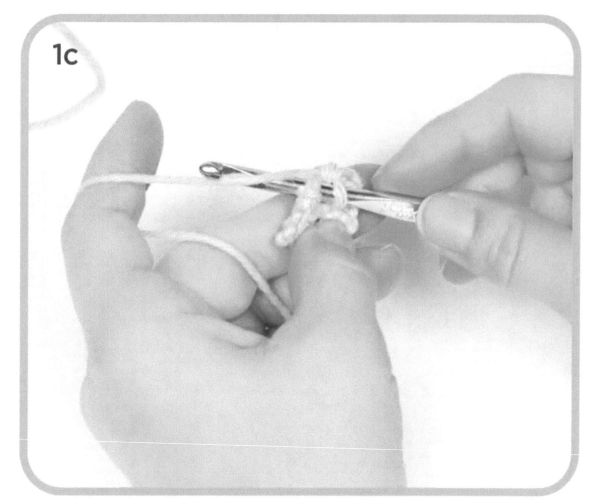

• Finish off, leaving a tail for sewing.

HEAD: Dark brown yarn
• Make adjustable ring.
Rnd 1: 6sc in ring (6)
Rnd 2: 2sc in each st (12)
Rnd 3: *2sc in next st, 1sc* (18)
Rnd 4: *2sc in next st, (1sc) 2x* (24)
Rnd 5: *2sc in next st, (1sc) 3x* (30)
Rnd 6: *2sc in next st, (1sc) 4x* (36)
Rnds 7–11: 1sc in each st (36)
Rnd 12: *2sc in next st, (1sc) 5x* (42)
Rnds 13–16: 1sc in each st (42)
Rnd 17: *sc2tog, (1sc) 5x* (36)
Rnd 18: *sc2tog, (1sc) 4x* (30)
Rnd 19: *sc2tog, (1sc) 3x* (24)
Rnd 20: *sc2tog, (1sc) 2x* (18)

1. Place a pinch of stuffing behind the mouth and begin stitching the mouth in place using the leftover yarn tail. The bottom of the mouth should be level with Rnd 16 from the head. **(fig. 1d)**

2. Place the two eye pieces close together above the mouth.

3. Push the eye stems through both layers of yarn and fasten securely.

4. Stitch the eye pieces in place using the leftover yarn tails. **(fig. 1e)**

1e

5. Using leftover yarn tails, stitch the ears in place on opposite sides of the head.

6. Stuff the head firmly, then pick up your working yarn where you left off after Rnd 20.

Rnd 21: *sc2tog, 1sc* (12)

Rnd 22: *sc2tog* (6)

• Finish off, weaving the leftover tail inside the head.

ARMS (MAKE 2): Tan yarn

• Make adjustable ring.

Rnd 1: 6sc in ring (6)

Rnd 2: *2sc in next st, 1sc (2x)* (8)

Rnd 3: *2sc in next st, 1sc* (12)
Rnds 4–5: 1sc in each st (12)
• Change yarn color to dark brown.
Rnds 6–7: 1sc in each st (12)
Rnd 8: *sc2tog, 1sc* (8)
Rnds 9–20: 1sc in each st (8)
• Finish off, leaving a tail for sewing.

LEGS (MAKE 2): Tan yarn
• Make adjustable ring.
Rnd 1: 6sc in ring (6)
Rnd 2: *2sc in next st, 1sc (2x)* (8)
Rnd 3: *2sc in next st, 1sc* (12)
Rnd 4: *2sc in next st, 1sc (2x)* (16)
Rnds 5–6: 1sc in each st (16)
• Change yarn color to dark brown. **(fig. 1f)**

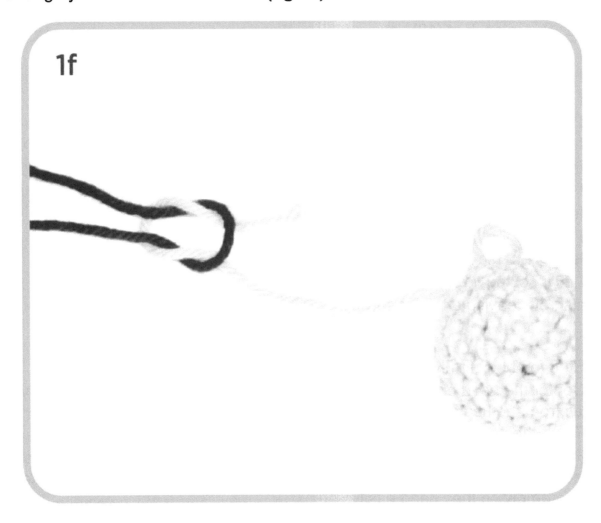

1f

Rnd 7: 1sc in each st (16)
Rnd 8: *sc2tog, 1sc (2x)* (12)
Rnds 9–13: 1sc in each st (12)
Rnd 14: *sc2tog, 1sc (4x)* (10)
Rnds 15–24: 1sc in each st (10)
• Finish off, leaving a tail for sewing.

TAIL: Dark brown yarn
• Make adjustable ring.
Rnd 1: 6sc in ring (6)
Rnd 2: *2sc in next st, 1sc (2x)* (8)
Rnds 3–27: 1sc in each st (8)
• Finish off, leaving a tail for sewing.

BODY: Dark brown yarn
• Make adjustable ring.
Rnd 1: 6sc in ring (6)
Rnd 2: 2sc in each st (12)
Rnd 3: *2sc in next st, 1sc* (18)
Rnd 4: *2sc in next st, (1sc) 2x* (24)
Rnd 5: *2sc in next st, (1sc) 3x* (30)
Rnd 6: 1sc in each st (30)
Rnd 7: *2sc in next st, (1sc) 4x* (36)
Rnds 8–11: 1sc in each st (36)
Rnd 12: *sc2tog, (1sc) 4x* (30)
Rnds 13–16: 1sc in each st (30)
Rnd 17: *sc2tog, (1sc) 3x* (24)
Rnds 18–19: 1sc in each st (24)
Rnd 20: *sc2tog, (1sc) 2x* (18)
• Finish off, leaving a tail for sewing.

FINISHING:
1. Stuff the body firmly.
2. Center the head on top of the body and stitch in place using the leftover yarn tail from the body.
3. Pinch the arms flat and stitch in place at shoulder level, just below the neck.
4. Push small amounts of stuffing into the legs, working the stuffing down to the feet—stuffing should only be in the feet up to Rnd 13. After that, leave the legs empty so they bend easily.

5. Stitch the legs in place using the leftover yarn tails.

6. Stitch the tail in place on the backside using leftover yarn tail.

7. Weave in all ends.

project **2**

COW

FROM DENISE FERGUSON IN PENNS YLVANIA

Designer Denise Ferguson specializes in food items, but she made this deliciously cute cow just for us. And these guys are easy to corral! Pretty perfect, huh?

what you'll need:

- G/6 (4.0 mm) crochet hook
- worsted weight yarn in white, black, pink, dark pink, and brown
- black safety eyes (9 mm)
- chenille needle
- stuffing

FINISHED SIZE: About 5 inches tall

Instructions

EARS (MAKE 2): Black yarn
• Make adjustable ring.
Rnd 1: 6sc in ring (6)
Rnd 2: *1sc, 2sc in next st* (9)
Rnd 3: *(1sc) 2x, 2sc in next st*(12)
Rnd 4: 1sc in each st (12)
Rnd 5: *(1sc) 2x, sc2tog* (9)
• Finish off, leaving a long tail for sewing.

HORNS (MAKE 2): Brown yarn
• Make adjustable ring.
Rnd 1: 6sc in ring (6)
Rnd 2: 1sc in each st (6)
• Finish off, leaving a long tail for sewing.

NOSTRILS (MAKE 2): Dark pink yarn
• Make adjustable ring.
Rnd 1: 6sc in ring (6)
• Finish off, leaving a long tail for sewing.

SNOUT: Pink yarn **(fig. 2a)**

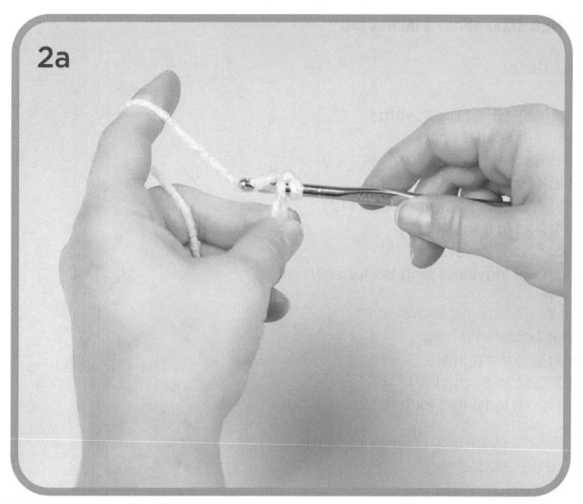

2a

Rnd 1: ch 8, 1sc in 2nd ch from hook, (1sc) 5x, 3sc in next st. Continuing around to the other side of your foundation row: (1sc) 5x, 2sc in next st (16)

Rnd 2: (1sc) 7x, 2sc in next st, (1sc) 7x, 2sc in next st (18)

Rnd 3: 1 sc in each st (18)

Rnd 4: 1sc in each st (18)

• Finish off, leaving a long tail for sewing.

• Sew on nostrils. **(fig. 2b)**

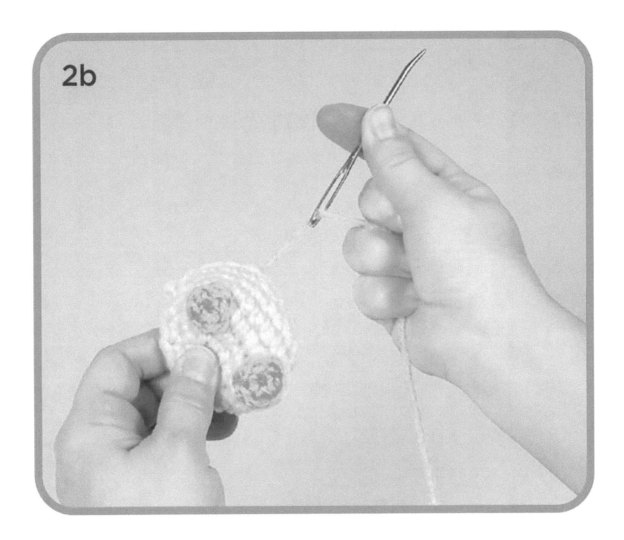

HEAD: White yarn
• Make adjustable ring.
Rnd 1: 6sc in ring (6)
Rnd 2: 2sc in each stitch (12)
Rnd 3: *1sc, 2sc in next st* (18)
Rnd 4: *(1sc) 2x, 2sc in next st* (24) **(fig. 2c)**

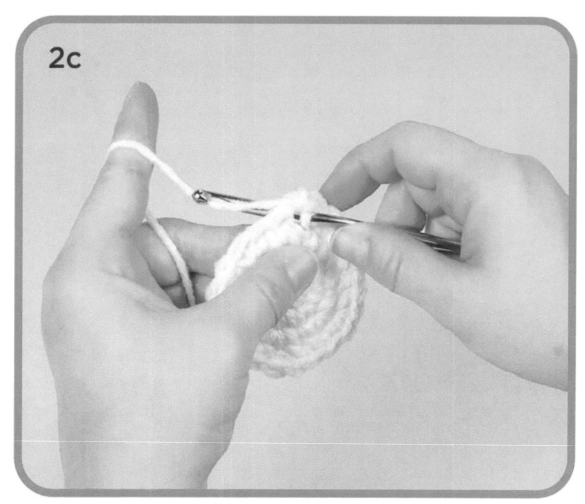

Rnd 5: *(1sc) 3x, 2sc in next st* (30)

Rnd 6: *(1sc) 4x, 2sc in next st* (36)

Rnds 7–11: 1 sc in each st (36)

• At this point, stop and sew on the ears and horns, add the safety eyes, and stuff and sew on the snout. **(fig. 2d)**

Rnd 12: *(1sc) 4x, sc2tog* (30)
Rnd 13: *(1sc) 3x, sc2tog* (24)
Rnd 14: *(1sc) 2x, sc2tog* (18)
Rnd 15: *1sc, sc2tog* (12)
Rnd 16: (sc2tog) 6x (6)
• Finish off, leaving a long tail for sewing.

LEGS (MAKE 4): Black yarn
• Make adjustable ring.
Rnd 1: 6sc in ring (6)
Rnd 2: 2sc in each stitch (12)
Rnd 3: In back loop, 1 sc in each st (12)
• Change to white yarn. **(fig. 2e)**

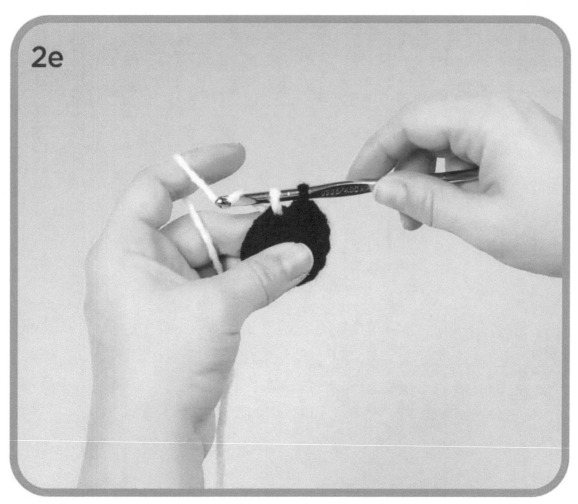

2e

Rnds 4–7: 1sc in each st (12)

• Finish off, leaving a long tail for sewing.

TAIL: White yarn

• Work in a row:

Row 1: ch 8, 1 sc in second ch from hook, (1sc) 6x (7)

• Finish off, leaving a long tail for sewing. Tie a few small pieces of black yarn to the other end. **(fig. 2f)**

2f

LITTLE SPOT (MAKE 2): Black yarn
• Make adjustable ring.
Rnd 1: 6sc in ring (6)
Rnd 2: (2sc in next st) 1x, (2hdc in next st) 2x, (2sc in next st) 3x (12)
• Finish off, leaving a long tail for sewing.

BIG SPOTS (MAKE 2): Black yarn
• Make adjustable ring.
Rnd 1: 6sc in ring (6)
Rnd 2: 2sc in each stitch (12)
Rnd 3: (1sc, 2sc in next st) 2x, (1hdc, 2hdc in next st) 2x, (1sc, 2sc in next st) 1x, (1hdc, 2hdc in next st) 1x (18) **(fig. 2g)**

2g

• Finish off, leaving a long tail for sewing.

BODY: White yarn
• Make adjustable ring.
Rnd 1: 6sc in ring (6)
Rnd 2: 2sc in each stitch (12)
Rnd 3: 1sc, 2sc in next st (18)
Rnd 4: *(1sc) 2x, 2sc in next st* (24)
Rnd 5: *(1sc) 3x, 2sc in next st* (30)
Rnd 6: *(1sc) 4x, 2sc in next st* (36)
Rnds 7–16: 1sc in each st (36)
Rnd 17: *(1sc) 4x, sc2tog* (30)
Rnd 18: *(1sc) 3x, sc2tog* (24)
Rnd 19: *(1sc) 2x, sc2tog* (18)
Rnd 20: *1sc, sc2tog* (12)
Rnd 21: (sc2tog) 6x (6)
• Finish off. Stuff and sew on the head and legs, then sew on spots and tail.

pig

FROM AMANDA C. SCOFIELD

Pigs are adorable—but they do love a good roll in the mud from time to time. Not this one, though! This little pink pig needs no cleaning, doesn't eat anything, and is always ready to cuddle.

what you'll need:

- **F/5 (3.75 mm) crochet hook**
- **worsted weight yarn in light pink and dark pink**

- **black safety eyes (9 mm)**
- **chenille needle**
- **stuffing**

FINISHED SIZE: About 6 inches tall

Instructions

BODY: Light pink yarn
- Make adjustable ring.
Rnd 1: 6sc in ring (6)
Rnd 2: 2sc in each stitch (12)
Rnd 3: *2sc in next st, 1sc* (18)
Rnd 4: *2sc in next st, 2sc* (24)
Rnd 5: *2sc in next st, 3sc* (30)
Rnd 6: *2sc in next st, 4sc* (36)
Rnd 7: *2sc in next st, 5sc* (42)
Rnd 8: *2sc in next st, 6sc* (48)
Rnds 9–16: sc in each st (48)
- Pause crocheting and attach safety eyes about 1 inch apart, between Rnds 8 and 9. **(fig. 3a)**

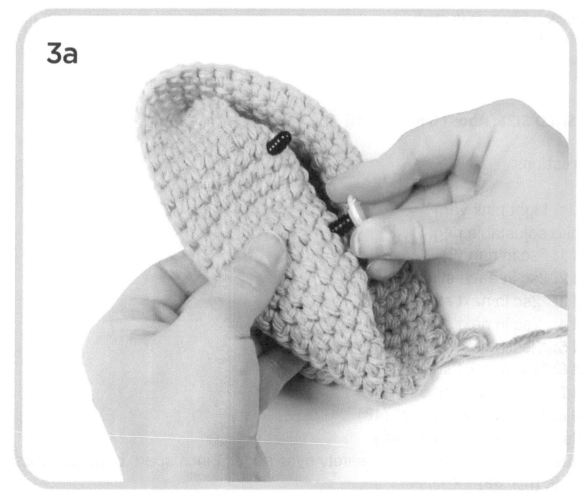

3a

Rnd 17: *sc2tog, 6sc* (42)
Rnd 18: *sc2tog, 5sc* (36)
Rnd 19: *sc2tog, 4sc* (30)
Rnd 20: *sc2tog, 3sc* (24)
• Pause crocheting and stuff body firmly.
• Pause between rounds from here to end, continuing to stuff the body until firm.
Rnd 21: *sc2tog, 2sc* (18)
Rnd 22: *sc2tog, sc* (12)
Rnd 23: sc2tog around (6)
• Finish off, leaving a long tail for sewing. Use yarn tail to sew the last round shut.

NOSE: Light pink yarn
• Make adjustable ring.
Rnd 1: 6sc in ring (6)
Rnd 2: 2sc in each stitch (12)
Rnd 3: *2sc in next st, 1sc* (18)

Rnd 4: 1sc in each st around, working in back loops only. (18) **(fig. 3b)**

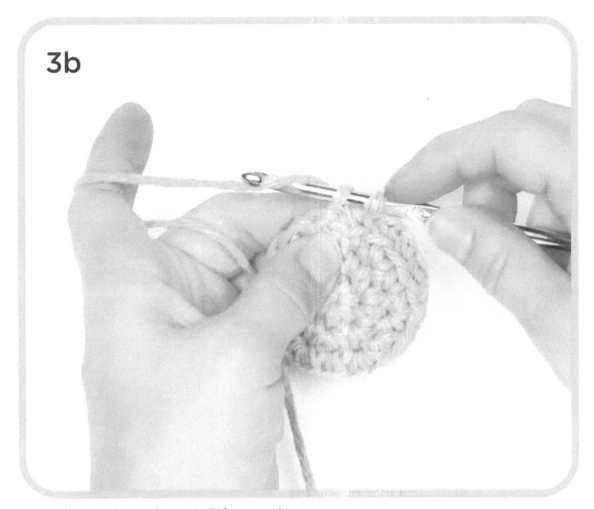

3b

• Finish off, leaving a long tail for sewing.
• Stuff lightly and sew to the body between and below the eyes.

LEGS (MAKE 4): Light pink yarn
• Make adjustable ring.
Rnd 1: 6sc in ring (6)
Rnd 2: (2sc in next st, 1sc) 3x (9)
Rnd 3: 1sc in each st around, working in back loops only (9)
Rnd 4: 1sc in each st around (9)
Rnd 5: (2sc in next st, 2sc) 3x (12)
Rnd 6: 1sc in each st around (12)
• Finish off, leaving a long tail for sewing. Stuff firmly and sew to the body. **(fig. 3c)**

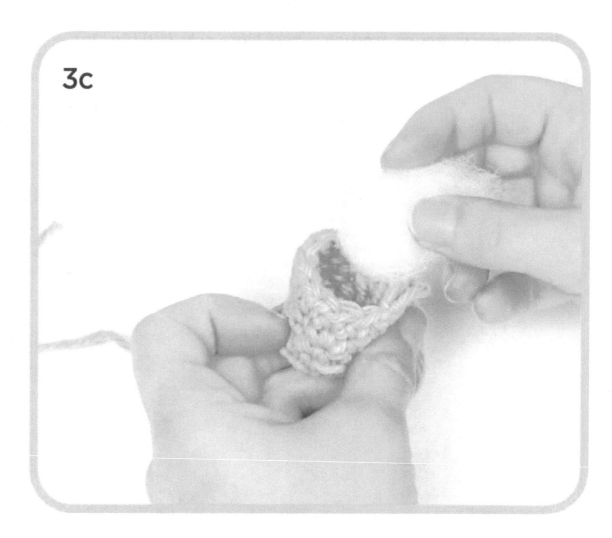

3c

OUTER EARS (MAKE 2): Light pink yarn

• Working in rows:

Row 1: ch 2, 2sc in 2nd chain from hook, ch 1, turn (2) **(fig. 3d)**

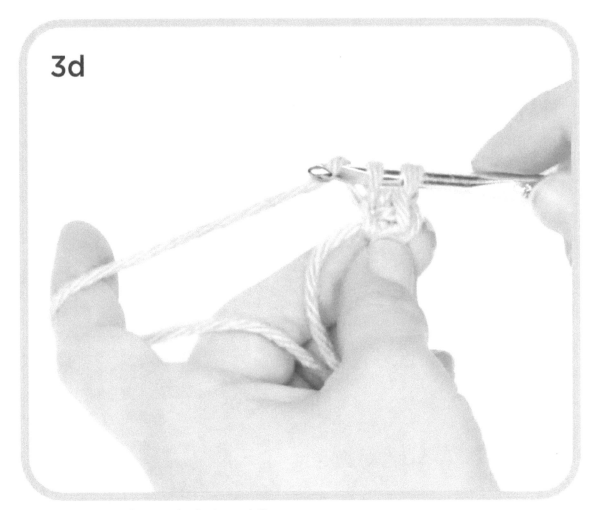

3d

Row 2: 2sc in each st, ch 1, turn (4)
Row 3: (2sc in next st, 1sc) 2x, ch 1, turn (6)
Row 4: (2sc in next st, 2sc) 2x, ch 1, turn (8)
Row 5: 2sc in first st, 6sc, 2sc in last st, ch 1, turn (10)
Row 6: 1sc in each st across (10)
• Finish off, leaving a long tail for sewing.

INNER EARS (MAKE 2): Dark pink yarn
• Working in rows:
Row 1: ch 2, 2sc in 2nd chain from hook, ch 1, turn (2) **(fig. 3e)**

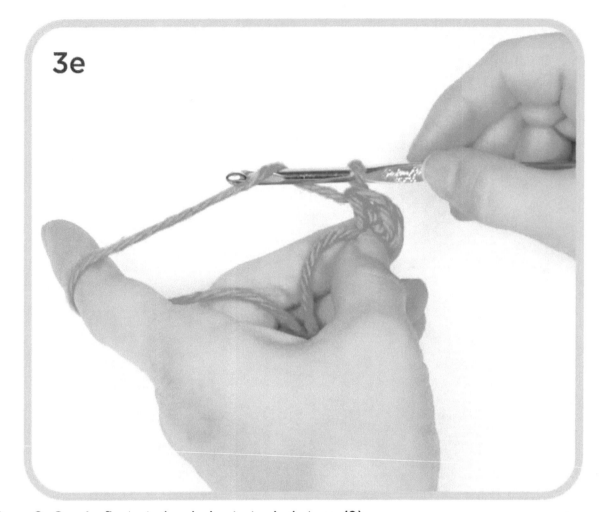

Row 2: 2sc in first st, 1sc in last st, ch 1, turn (3)

Row 3: 2sc in first st, 1sc, 2sc in last st, ch 1, turn (5)

Row 4: (1c) 2x, 2sc in next st, (1sc) 2x (6). Ch 1, turn

Row 5: sc in each st across (6)

• Finish off, leaving a long tail for sewing. Sew to the inside of the light pink outside of ear, then sew the finished ear to the body between Rnds 4 and 9.

TAIL: Light pink yarn

• Ch 7

• Working in back of chain, 2sc in 2nd chain from hook and in each chain bump across (12) **(fig. 3f)**

3f

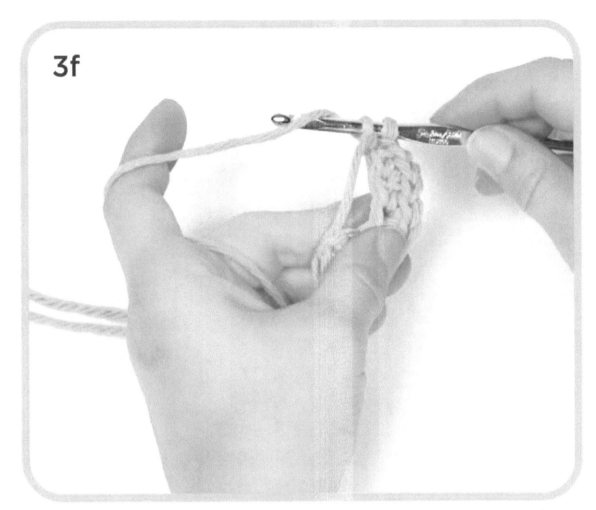

• Piece will curl back on itself. Finish off, leaving a long tail for sewing. Securely attach the tail to the back of the body between Rnds 6 and 7.

chick

FROM MADELYN IN ALABAMA

With its felt beak and waddly feet, this happy little chick designed by Madelyn is so cute you won't be able to stop at just one. You can make them quickly, and a flock of these would make great decorations for spring—your neighbors will quack up when they see these guys popping up in all your windows!

what you'll need:

• **F/5 (3.75 mm) crochet hook**

- worsted weight acrylic yarn in yellow and orange
- black safety eyes (6 mm)
- orange felt
- embroidery floss in orange
- chenille needle
- sewing needle
- stuffing

FINISHED SIZE: About 3$^1/_4$ inches tall

Instructions

HEAD: Yellow yarn
- Make adjustable ring.

Rnd 1: 6sc in ring (6)

Rnd 2: 2sc in each stitch (12)

Rnd 3: *1sc in next st, 2sc in next st* (18)

Rnd 4: *(1sc) 2x, 2sc in next st* (24)

Rnd 5: *(1sc) 3x, 2sc in next st* (30)

Rnds 6–10: 1sc in each stitch (30)

- Attach safety eyes on Rnd 9. **(fig. 4a)**

4a

Rnd 11: *sc2tog, 3sc* (24)
Rnd 12: *sc2tog, 2sc* (18)
Rnd 13: *sc2tog, 1sc* (12)
• Finish off, leaving a long tail for sewing. Stuff firmly.

BODY: Yellow yarn
• Make adjustable ring.
Rnd 1: 5sc in ring (5)
Rnd 2: 2sc in each stitch (10)
Rnd 3: *1sc in next st, 2sc in next st* (15)
Rnd 4: *(1sc) 2x, 2sc in next st* (20)
Rnds 5–6: 1sc in each stitch (20)
Rnd 7: *(sc2tog) 5x, 10sc* (15) **(fig. 4b)**

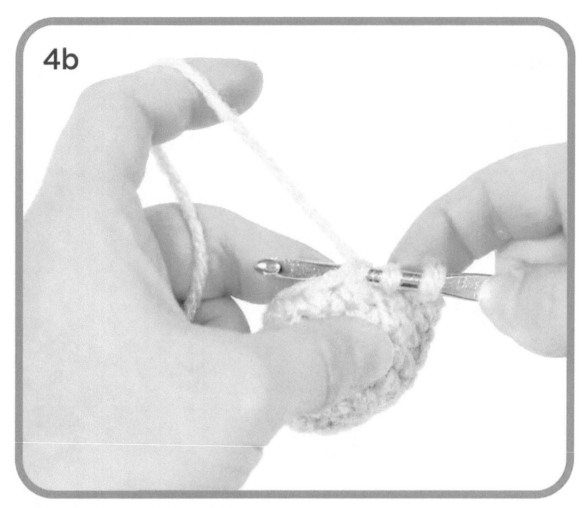

4b

Rnds 8–9: 1sc in each stitch (15)
Rnd 10: *6sc, (sc2tog, 1sc) 3x* (12)
• End with sl st. Finish off. Stuff firmly.

WINGS (MAKE 2): Yellow yarn
• Make adjustable ring.
Rnd 1: 6sc in ring (6)
Rnd 2: 2sc in each stitch (12)
Rnd 3: *1sc in next st, 2sc in next st* (18) **(fig. 4c)**

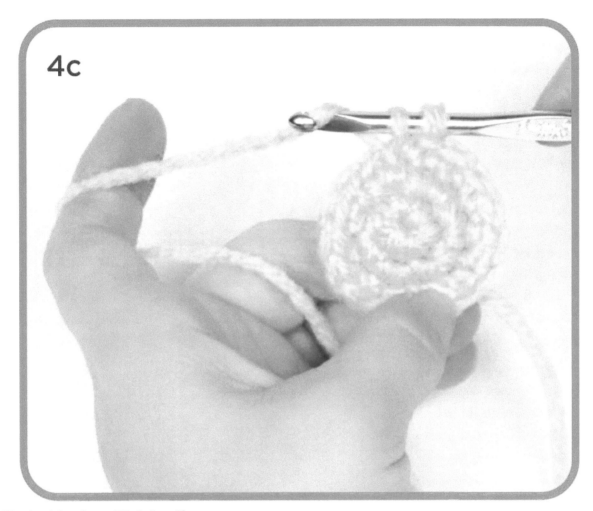

4c

• End with sl st. Finish off.

BEAK: Orange felt
• Using the template shown here, cut a beak shape from felt. Sew the beak in the middle of Rnd 10 using orange embroidery floss. **(fig. 4d)**

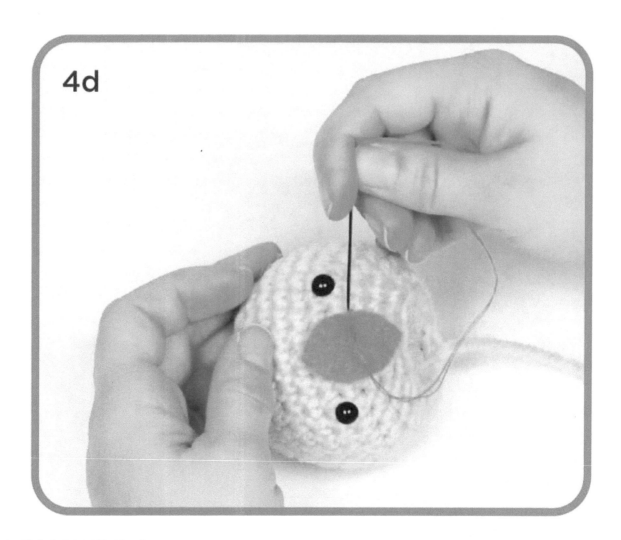

4d

FEET (MAKE 2): Orange yarn
• Make adjustable ring.
Rnd 1: 6sc in ring (6) **(fig. 4e)**

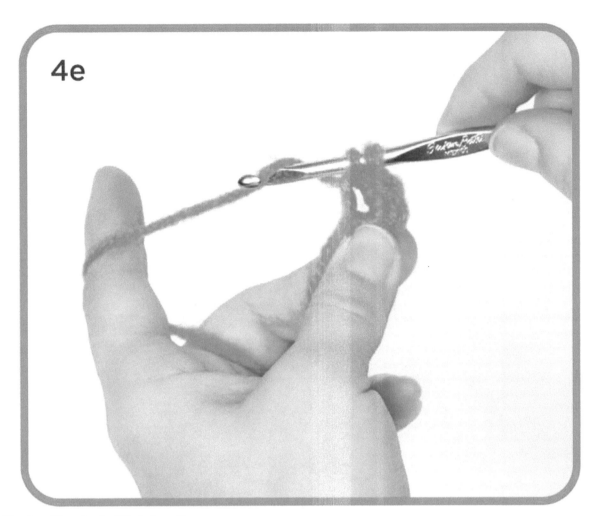

4e

• End with sl st. Finish off.

FINISHING:
  1. Sew the head to body. **(fig. 4f)**

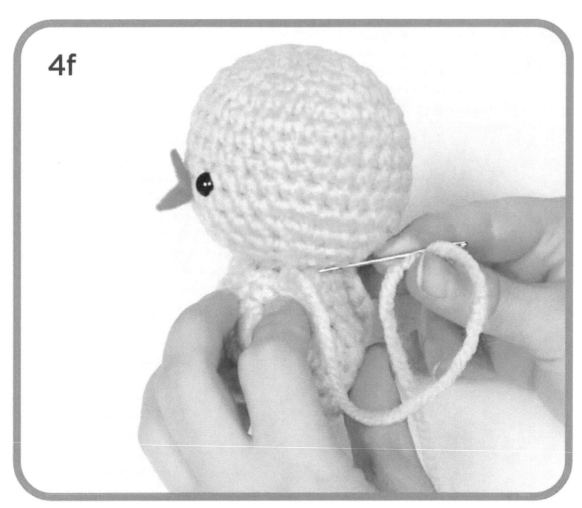

2. Sew a wing to each side of the body.

3. Sew the feet to the bottom of the body.

giraffe

FROM CELIA TSENG IN BALDWINSVILLE, NEW YORK

Celia has been crocheting since she was a girl, and now that she has kids of her own, she draws on her lifelong hobby to create new toys for them. Her patterns are sentimental and sweet, but also serious—this sassy giraffe stands on its own at a foot tall. Finish this project by adding heart spots wherever you like.

what you'll need:

- F/5 (3.75 mm) crochet hook
- worsted weight yarn in yellow and brown
- brown and black embroidery floss
- black safety eyes
- chenille needle
- stuffing

FINISHED SIZE: About 12 inches tall

Instructions

HEAD: Yellow yarn
- Make adjustable ring.
Rnd 1: 6sc in ring (6)
Rnd 2: *1sc in next st, 2sc in next st* (9)
Rnd 3: *(1sc) 2x, 2sc in next st* (12)
Rnd 4: *(1sc) 2x, 2sc in next st, 1sc* (15)
Rnd 5: *2sc in next st, (1sc) 4x* (18)
Rnd 6: *2sc in next st, (1sc) 2x* (24)
Rnd 7: *(1sc) 2x, 2sc in next st, 1sc* (30)
Rnd 8: *2sc in next st, (1sc) 4x* (36)
Rnd 9–12: 1sc in each stitch (36)
- Insert safety eyes at Rnd 6.
- Use embroidery floss to sew the nose on Rnd 1 and the mouth on Rnd 3.
Rnd 13: *sc2tog, (1sc) 4x* (30)
Rnd 14: 1sc in each stitch (30)
Rnd 15: *(1sc) 2x, sc2tog, 1sc* (24)
Rnd 16: *sc2tog, (1sc) 2x * (18) **(fig. 5a)**

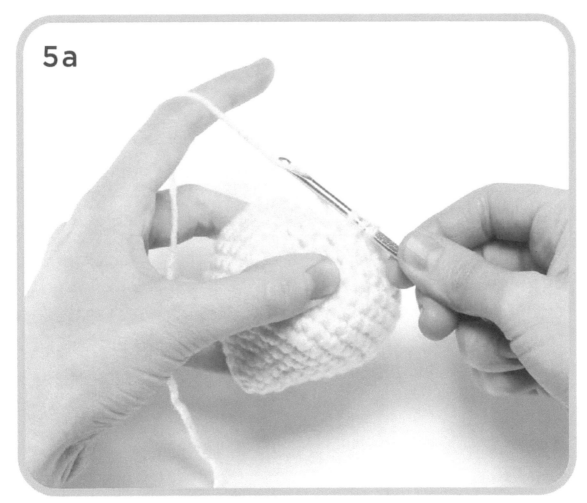

5a

• Pause crocheting and begin stuffing.

Rnd 17: *sc2tog, 1sc* (12)

Rnd 18: *sc2tog* (6)

• Finish stuffing and close with sl st, leaving a long tail for sewing.

BODY: Yellow yarn

• Make adjustable ring.

Rnd 1: 6sc in ring (6)

Rnd 2: 2sc in each stitch (12)

Rnd 3: *1sc, 2sc in next st* (18)

Rnd 4: *2sc in next st, (1sc) 2x* (24)

Rnd 5: *(1sc) 2x, 2sc in next st, 1sc* (30)

Rnd 6: *2sc in next st, (1sc) 4x* (36)

Rnd 7: *(1sc) 3x, 2sc in next st, (1sc) 2x* (42)

Rnd 8–16: 1sc in each stitch (42)

Rnd 17: *(1sc) 3x, sc2tog, (1sc) 2x* (36)

Rnd 18: *sc2tog, (1sc) 4x* (30)

Rnd 19: *(1sc) 2x, sc2tog, 1sc* (24)
Rnd 20: *sc2tog, (1sc) 2x* (18)
• Pause crocheting and begin stuffing.
Rnd 21: *1sc, sc2tog* (12)
Rnd 22: *sc2tog* (6)
• Finish stuffing and close with sl st, leaving a long tail for sewing.

NECK: Yellow yarn

• Leave a longer tail on the starting slip knot to use for sewing later.
• Foundation row: ch 24, sc in the first st to make a loop, 1sc
Rnd 1: 1sc in each stitch (24)
Rnd 2: *(1sc) 2x, sc2tog* (18)
Rnd 3: 1sc in each stitch (18)
Rnd 4: *1sc, sc2tog* (12)
Rnd 5–13: 1sc in each stitch (12) **(fig. 5b)**

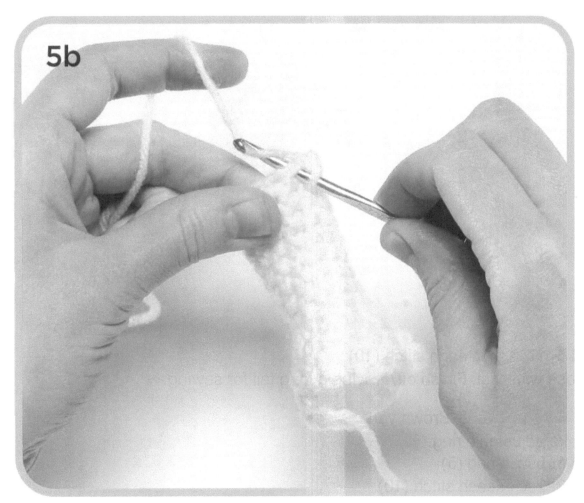

• Finish off, leaving a long tail for sewing.

LEGS (MAKE 4): Brown yarn

• Make adjustable ring.
Rnd 1: 6sc in ring (6)
Rnd 2: 2sc in each stitch (12)
Rnd 3: 1sc in each stitch (12)
Rnd 4: *sc2tog, (1sc) 4x* (10)

• Switch to yellow yarn. **(fig. 5c)**

Rnd 5–17: 1sc in each stitch (10)
• Close with sl st. Finish off, leaving a long tail for sewing.

HORNS (MAKE 2): Brown yarn
• Make adjustable ring.
Rnd 1: 5sc in ring (5)
Rnd 2: 2sc in each stitch (10)
Rnd 3: 1sc in each stitch (10)
Rnd 4: *sc2tog, (1sc) 3x* (8)
• Switch to yellow yarn.
Rnd 5–6: 1sc in each stitch (7)
• Finish off, leaving a long tail for sewing, and stuff.

TAIL: Yellow yarn
• Make adjustable ring.
Rnd 1: 5sc in ring. (5)

Rnd 2–9: 1sc in each stitch (5) **(fig. 5d)**

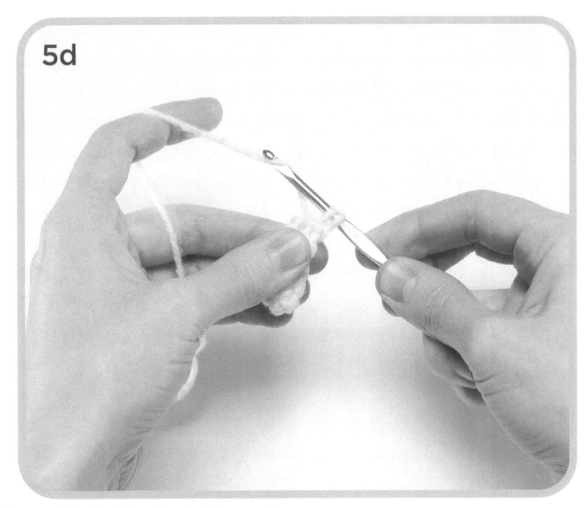

• Close with sl st, leaving tail for sewing.

EARS (MAKE 2): Yellow yarn
• Make adjustable ring.
Rnd 1: 6sc in ring (6)
Rnd 2: 1sc in each stitch (6)
Rnd 3: 2sc in each stitch (12)
Rnd 4: 1sc in each stitch (12)
Rnd 5: *sc2tog, (1sc) 4x* (10)
Rnd 6: 1sc in each stitch (10)
• Finish off, leaving a long tail for sewing.

HEART SPOTS (MAKE 4): Brown yarn
• Make adjustable ring.
• 1sc in ring (ch 3, tr in ring, ch 2, sc in ring, ch 2, tr in ring, ch 3) **(fig. 5e and 5f)**

5e

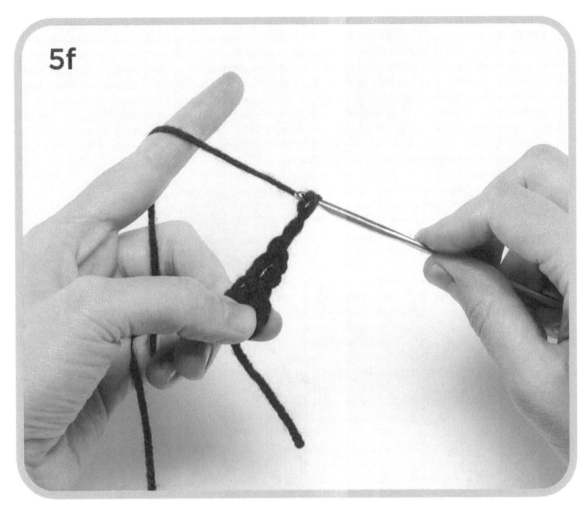

• Close with sl st through first sc, leaving tail for sewing.

FINISHING:
  1. Sew the neck to the head around Rnds 9–12. Stuff the neck well.
  2. Sew the neck to the body starting at Rnd 8. Add stuffing to the neck as needed so it will stay up by itself.
  3. Stuff the legs and sew onto the body about 2 stitches apart from each other.
  4. Sew tail on the center back of the body. Cut 4 pieces of brown yarn and tie them to the end of the tail: chain through stitches at end of the tail, knot.
  5. Sew the horns on top of the head at Rnd 10 of the head, 2 stitches apart.
  6. Sew the flattened ears on top of the head next to the horns.
  7. Sew heart spots on body as desired.

project **6**

bird

FROM AMANDA LYNN IN WILHITE, WISCONSIN

This little mama bird is watching over her babies until they are all hatched. Once you start making these, you'll start designing your own color patterns, and soon will have a whole flock!

what you'll need:

- **E/4 (3.5 mm), F/5 (3.75 mm), and I/9 (5.5 mm) crochet hooks**
- **worsted weight yarn in blue, white and yellow**
- **bulky yarn in brown**
- **2 pairs of black safety eyes (4 mm and 6 mm)**
- **chenille needle**
- **stuffing**

FINISHED SIZE: Mama Bird: About 3 inches tall. Baby Birdie and Eggs: About 1 inch tall. Nest: About 3 inches in diameter.

Instructions

MAMA BIRD

HEAD: Start with blue yarn

• Using F/5 hook, make an adjustable ring.

Rnd 1: 6sc into ring (6)

Rnd 2: 2sc in each st (12)

Rnd 3: *1sc, 2sc in next st* (18)

Rnd 4: *2sc, 2sc in next st* (24)

Rnd 5–7: 1sc in each st. Leave 2 loops on hook in last st to change to White yarn. (24)

Rnd 8–10: 1sc in each st (24) **(fig. 6a)**

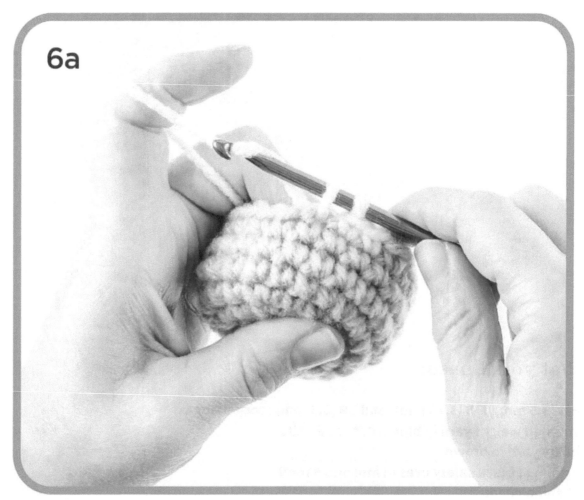

• Attach the 6 mm safety eyes, between Rounds 7 and 8.

• Stitch the beak between Rounds 7 and 10 with the yellow yarn.
Rnd 11: *2sc, sc2tog* (18) **(fig. 6b)**

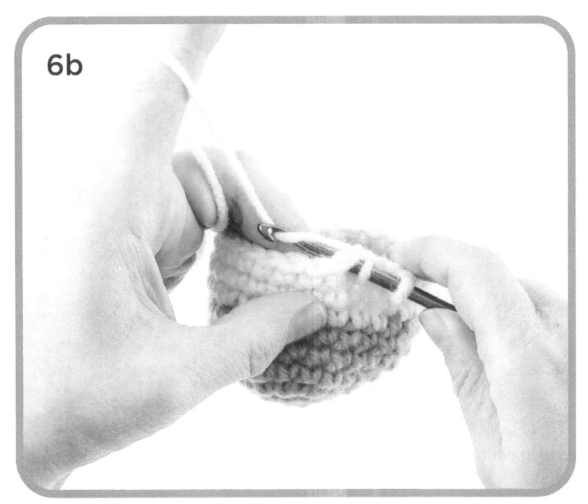

6b

• Stuff the head firmly.
Rnd 12: *1sc, sc2tog* (12)
Rnd 13: *1sc2tog* (6)
• Finish off, leaving a long tail to make the loops on the top of the head.
• Pull the yarn tail up through the top of the bird's head and loop it over your pinky through the bottom of the bird's head repeating 3 times for 3 loops. **(fig. 6c)**

6c

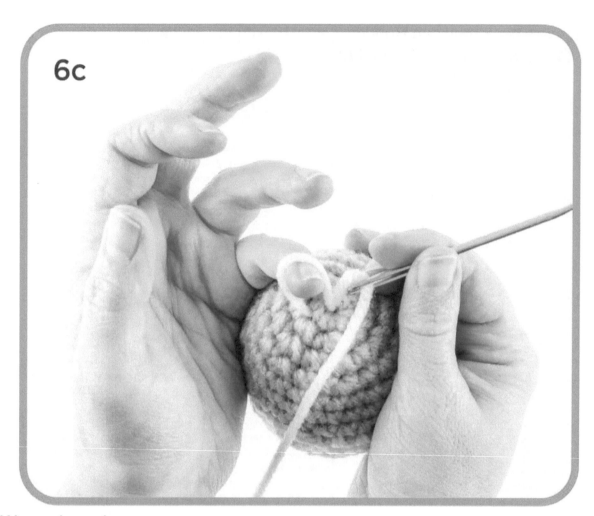

• Weave in ends.

BODY: Blue yarn

• Using F hook, make an adjustable ring.

Rnd 1: 7sc into ring (7)

Rnd 2: 2sc in each st (14)

Rnd 3–5: 1sc in each st (14)

Rnd 6: *1sc, sc2tog* 4x, 2sc (10) **(fig. 6d)**

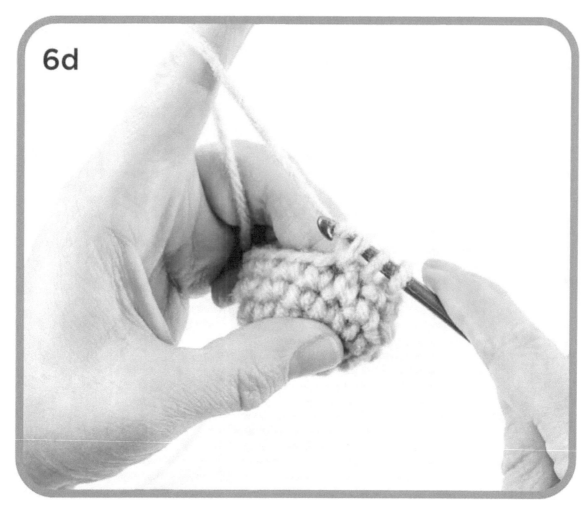

6d

- Finish off, leaving a long tail.
- Sew bird's feet with yellow yarn.
- Stuff body and sew to head.

WINGS (MAKE 2): Blue yarn
- Using F hook, make an adjustable ring.
Rnd 1: 6sc into ring (6)
Rnd 2: 2sc in each of next 3 sts, leave last 3 st unworked (9) **(fig. 6e)**

6e

- Finish off, leaving a long tail.
- Sew wings to body.

TAIL: Blue yarn
- Using F hook, make an adjustable ring.
Rnd 1: 5sc into ring (5)
Rnd 2: 2sc in each st (10)
Rnd 3: sc in each st (10)
- Finish off, leaving a tail for sewing.
- Sew end closed and sew to body.

BABY BIRDIE: Blue yarn
- Using E hook, make an adjustable ring.
Rnd 1: 6sc into ring (6)
Rnd 2: *1sc, 2sc in next st* (9)
Rnd 3–4: 1sc in each st (9)
- Finish off, leaving a long tail.

• Attach the 4mm safety eyes between rounds 2 and 3, and center beak between the eyes and sew with yellow yarn. Stuff body with stuffing. **(fig. 6f)**

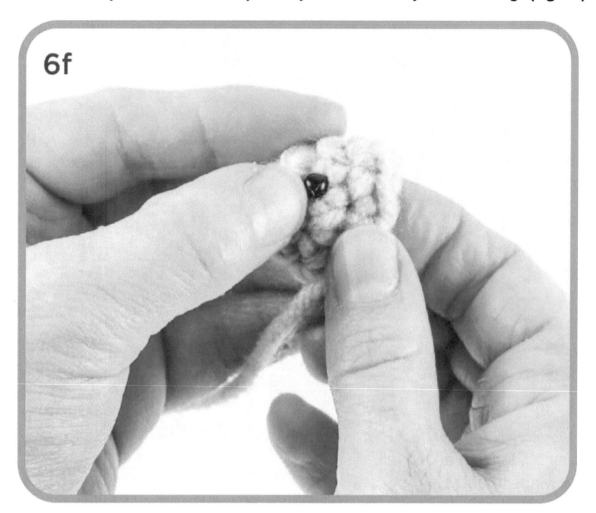

6f

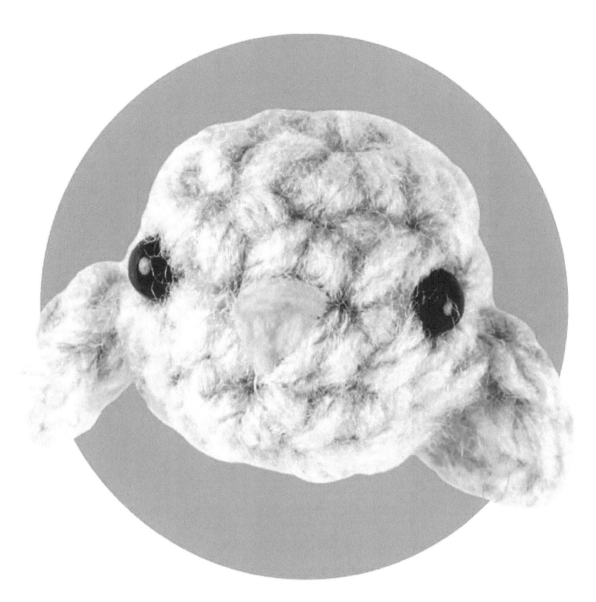

BABY BIRDIE WINGS (MAKE 2): Blue yarn
• Using E hook, make an adjustable ring.
Rnd1: 5sc into ring (5)
• Finish off, leaving a long tail.
• Sew to baby birdie. **(fig. 6g)**

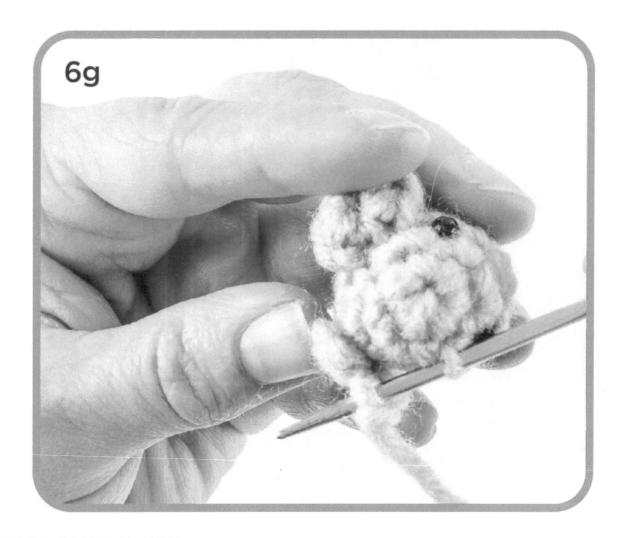

6g

EGGS (MAKE 2): White yarn
- Using E hook, make an adjustable ring.
Rnd 1: 6sc into ring (6)
Rnd 2: *sc, 2sc in next st* (9)
Rnd 3–4: sc in each st (9)
- Stuff egg.
Rnd 5: *sc, sc2tog* (6)
- Finish off, using the tail to close the egg. Weave in ends.

NEST: Brown yarn
- Using I hook, make an adjustable ring.
Rnd 1: 6sc into ring (6)
Rnd 2: 2sc in each st (12)
Rnd 3: *1sc, 2sc in next st* (18)
Rnd 4: *2sc, 2sc in next st* (24)
Rnd 5: *3sc, 2sc in next st* (30)

Rnd 6–8: sc in each st (30)

• Finish off and weave in ends.

koala

FROM KANDICE SORAYA IN CALIFORNIA

Koalas have been Kandice's favorite animal since childhood. This little guy is just as cute as the real thing, but he doesn't smell of eucalyptus and his claws aren't sharp! One of these would make a perfect gift for any koala lover.

what you'll need:

- G/6 (4.0 mm) crochet hook
- worsted weight yarn in heather gray and white

- **black felt**
- **black embroidery threead**
- **black safety eyes (6 mm)**
- **chenille needle**
- **embroidery needle**
- **stuffing**

FINISHED SIZE: About 4¹/₂ inches tall

Instructions

OUTER EARS (MAKE 2): Gray yarn
- Make adjustable ring.

Rnd 1: 6sc in ring (6)

Rnd 2: 2sc in each stitch (12)

Rnd 3: *2sc in next stitch, 1sc* (18)

Rnd 4: *2sc in next stitch, 2sc* (24)

Rnds 5–6: 1sc in each st (24)

- Close with sl st, leaving a long tail for sewing.
- Fold in half and use the tail to sew the ear shut. Leave the tail long to use for sewing again later. **(fig. 7a)**

7a

INNER EARS (MAKE 2): White yarn

• Make adjustable ring.

Rnd 1: 6sc in ring (6)

Rnd 2: 2sc in each stitch (12)

• Close with sl st, leaving a tail for sewing. Sew the entire piece into the outer ear.

• After the inner ear has been sewn into the outer ear, thread the needle with white yarn. Insert the needle into the inner ear and pull the yarn through until there is a 1-inch tail. Cut the other end of the yarn piece so you have about an inch on each side of the stitch. Tie the ends together so there is a knot at the base. Repeat, covering the entire inner ear with 1-inch strands. Then, use the needle to separate the strands to give the inner ear a fuzzy look. Trim inner ear fuzz to your desired length. **(fig. 7b)**

7b

BODY: Gray yarn
• Make adjustable ring.
Rnd 1: 6sc in ring (6)
Rnd 2: 2sc in each stitch (12) **(fig. 7c)**

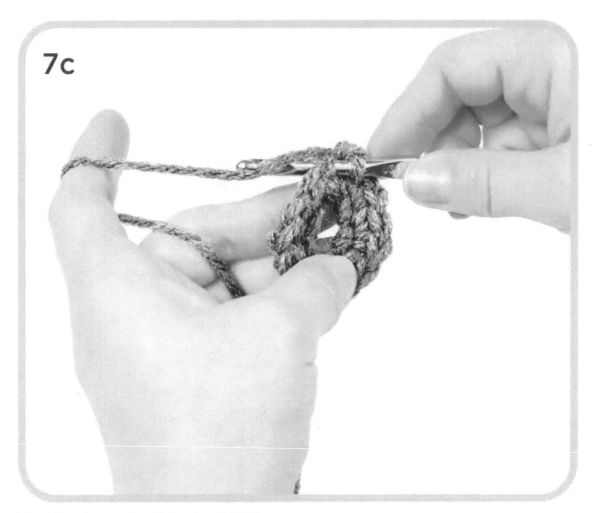

Rnd 3: *2sc in next stitch, 1sc* (18)
Rnd 4: *2sc in next stitch, 2sc* (24)
Rnds 5–7: 1sc in each st (24)
Rnd 8: *sc2tog, 6sc* (21)
Rnd 9: *sc2tog, 5sc* (8)
Rnd 10: *sc2tog, 4sc* (15)
• Begin stuffing the body.
Rnd 11: *sc2tog, 3sc* (12)
Rnd 12: *sc2tog, 2sc* (9)
Rnd 13: *sc2tog, 1sc* (6)
• Finish stuffing and close with sl st.

HEAD: Gray yarn
• Make adjustable ring.
Rnd 1: 6sc in ring (6)
Rnd 2: 2sc in each stitch (12)
Rnd 3: *2sc in next stitch, 1sc* (18)

Rnd 4: *2sc in next stitch, 2sc* (24)
Rnd 5: *2sc in next stitch, 3sc* (30)
Rnd 6: *2sc in next stitch, 4sc* (36)
Rnd 7: *2sc in next stitch, 5sc* (42)
Rnds 8–13: 1sc in each stitch (42)
• Pause crocheting. Attach safety eyes between Rnds 8 and 9, 6 stitches apart.
Rnd 14: *sc2tog, 5sc* (36)
Rnd 15: *sc2tog, 4sc* (30)
Rnd 16: *sc2tog, 3sc* (24)
Rnd 17: *sc2tog, 2sc* (18)
• Pause crocheting and stuff firmly.
Rnd 18: *sc2tog, 1sc* (12)
Rnd 19: 1sc in each stitch (12)
• Close with sl st, leaving a tail for sewing.

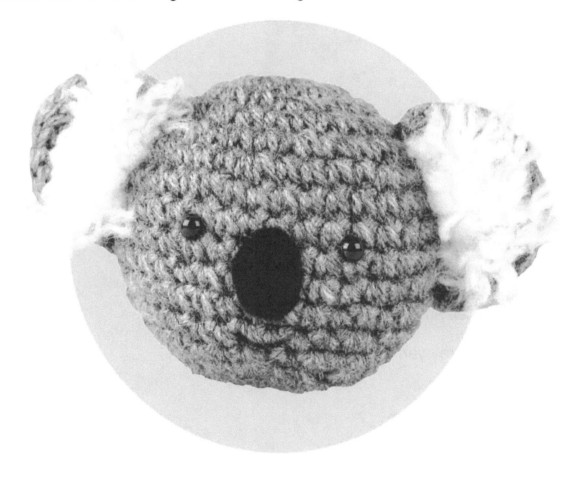

ARMS (MAKE 2): Gray yarn
• Make adjustable ring.
Rnd 1: 4sc in ring (4)
Rnd 2: 2sc in each stitch (8)

Rnds 3–4: 1sc in each stitch (8)
• Pause crocheting and stuff firmly. **(fig. 7d)**

Rnd 5: *sc2tog, 2sc* (6)
Rnds 6–8: 1sc in each st (6)
Rnd 9: *sc2tog, 1sc* (4)
• Close with sl st, leaving a tail for sewing.

LEGS (MAKE 2): Gray yarn
• Make adjustable ring.
Rnd 1: 6sc in ring (6)
Rnd 2: 2sc in each stitch (12)
Rnds 3–4: 1sc in each stitch (12)
• Pause crocheting and stuff firmly.
Rnd 5: *sc2tog, 4sc* (10)
Rnd 6: *sc2tog, 3sc* (8)
Rnd 7: 1sc in each stitch (8)

Rnd 8: *sc2tog, 2sc* (6)
• Close with sl st, leaving a tail for sewing.

FINISHING:

1. Align the head and body and sew together. **(fig. 7e)**

2. Sew the ears to the top of the head.
3. Sew the arms to the side of the body and the legs to the bottom of the base.
4. Use the template shown here to cut a nose from black felt. Sew on nose using embroidery thread, aligning the top of the nose with the eyes. **(fig. 7f)**

7f

5. Embroider a smile under the nose.
6. Embroider three stitches on each of the paws. **(fig. 7g)**

7g

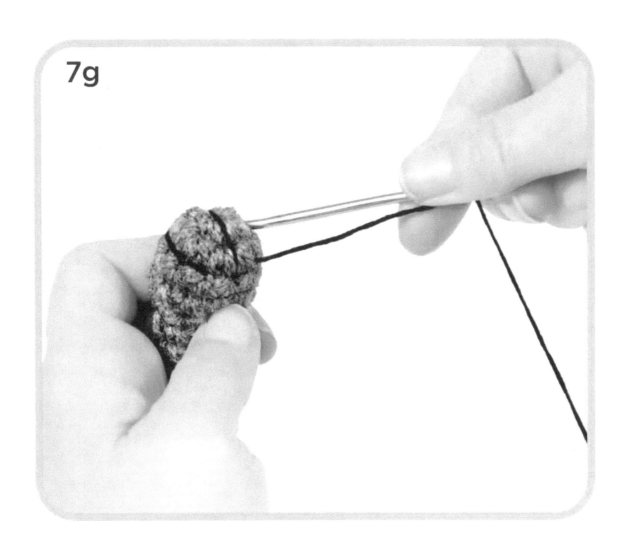

bear pod

FROM SWEEES IN THE U.S.A.

Part animal and part hidden container, this fuzzy hide-away is the perfect place to keep your house keys, or a couple of extra stitch markers. Sweees loves making patterns that are as innovative as they are adorable. Try personalizing this sweet bear pod by swapping in your favorite colors.

what you'll need:

- H/8 (5.0 mm) crochet hook
- worsted weight yarn in light blue, light green, antique white, and brown
- black safety eyes (12 mm)
- chenille needle
- button
- stuffing

FINISHED SIZE: About 5 inches tall

Instructions

EARS (MAKE 2): Light blue yarn
- Make adjustable ring.
Rnd 1: 6sc in ring (6)
Rnd 2: 2sc in each stitch (12)
Rnd 3: *2sc in next st, 1sc* (18)
Rnd 4: *2sc in next st, 2sc* (24)
- Close with sl st, leaving tail for sewing. Use antique white yarn to embroider ear detail on half the circle. **(fig. 8a)** Fold ear in half and use some of the light blue yarn tail to sew shut.

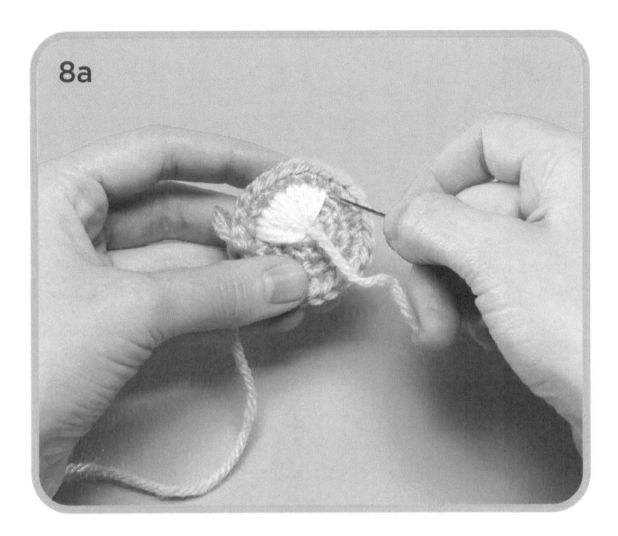

8a

NOSE: Antique white yarn

• Make adjustable ring.

Rnd 1: 6sc in ring (6)

Rnd 2: 2sc in each stitch (12)

Rnd 3: *2sc in next st, 2sc* (16)

Rnd 4: 1sc in each st (16)

• Close with sl st, leaving tail for sewing. Use brown yarn to sew on a mouth and nose between Rnd 11 and 17. **(fig. 8b)**

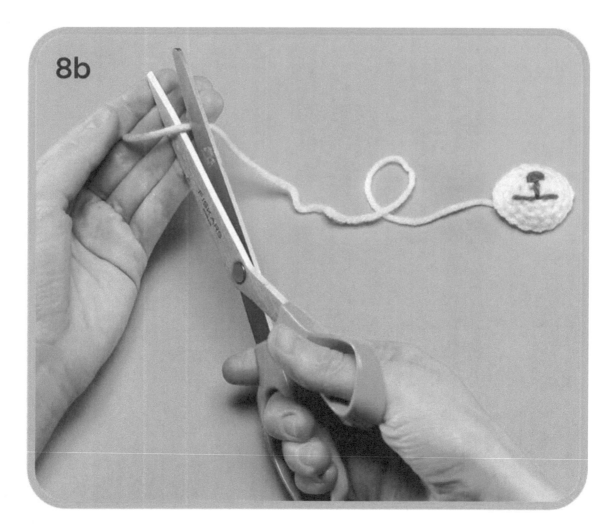

HEAD: Light blue yarn

• Make adjustable ring.

Rnd 1: 6sc in ring

Rnd 2: 2sc in each stitch (12)

Rnd 3: *2sc in next st, 1sc* (18)

Rnd 4: *2sc in next st, 2sc* (24)

Rnd 5: *2sc in next st, 3sc* (30)

Rnd 6: *2sc in next st, 4sc* (36)

Rnd 7: *2sc in next st, 5sc* (42)

Rnd 8: *2sc in next st, 6sc* (48)

Rnd 9: *2sc in next st, 7sc* (54)

Rnd 10–18: 1sc in each stitch (54)

• Attach safety eyes between Rnd 12 and 13, and sew on nose and ears.

Rnd 19: 1sc in back loops only (54) **(fig. 8c)**

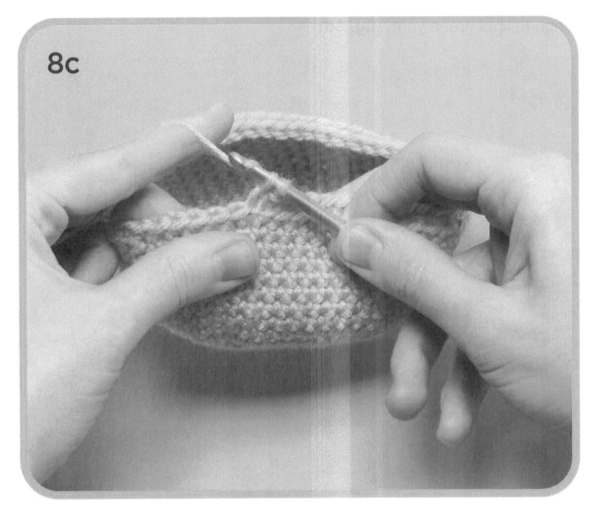

8c

Rnd 20: *sc2tog, 7sc* (48)
Rnd 21: 1sc in front loops only (48)
Rnd 22: *sc2tog, 6sc* in back loops only (42)
Rnd 23: *sc2tog, 5sc* (36)
Rnd 24: *sc2tog, 4sc* (30)
Rnd 25: *sc2tog, 3sc* (24)
• Begin stuffing, making sure the bottom is flat. Do not overstuff.
Rnd 26: *sc2tog, 2sc* (18)
Rnd 27: *sc2tog, 1sc* (12)
Rnd 28: *skip one st, 1sl st in next st*
• Close with sl st and weave in ends.

ARMS (MAKE 2): Light blue yarn
• Make adjustable ring.
Rnd 1: 4sc in ring
Rnd 2: 2sc in each stitch (8)
Rnd 3–5: 1sc in each stitch (8)

• Change to light green yarn. **(fig. 8d)**

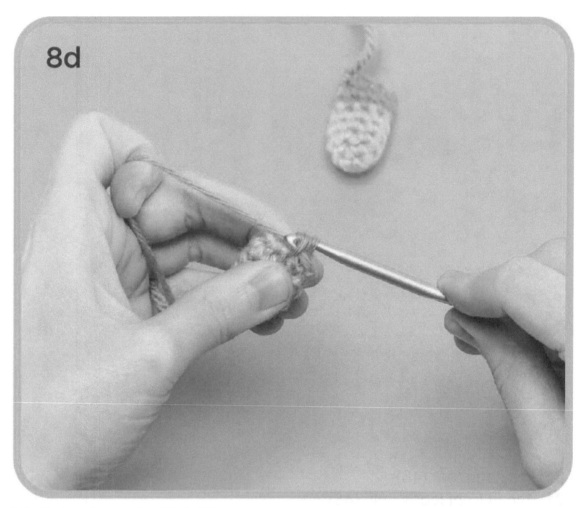

Rnd 6–7: 1sc in each stitch (8)
• Close with sl st, leaving tail for sewing. Stuff the tips of arms and sew the opening shut.

FEET (MAKE 2): Light blue yarn
• Make adjustable ring.
Rnd 1: 6sc in ring.
Rnd 2: 2sc in each stitch (12)
Rnd 3–6: 1sc in each stitch (12)
Rnd 7: *sc2tog, 4sc* (10)
• Close with sl st, leaving tail for sewing
• Stuff the tips of the feet and sew the opening shut.

TAIL: Light blue yarn

• Make adjustable ring.

Rnd 1: 5sc in ring

Rnd 2: 2sc in each stitch (10)

Rnd 3–4: 1sc in each stitch (10)

Rnd 5: *sc2tog, 3sc* (8)

• Close with sl st, leaving tail for sewing.

• Stuff tail and sew the opening shut.

BODY: Light green yarn

• Make adjustable ring.

Rnd 1: 6sc in ring

Rnd 2: 2sc in each stitch (12)

Rnd 3: *2sc in next st, 1sc* (18)

Rnd 4: *2sc in next st, 2sc* (24)

Rnd 5: *2sc in next st, 3sc* (30)

Rnd 6: *2sc in next st, 4sc* (36)

Rnd 7: *2sc in next st, 5sc* (42)

Rnd 8: *2sc in next st, 6sc* (48)

Rnd 9–17: 1sc in each stitch (48)

• Invert the piece. You've made the inside of the bowl. **(fig. 8e)** Continue crocheting to craft the outside.

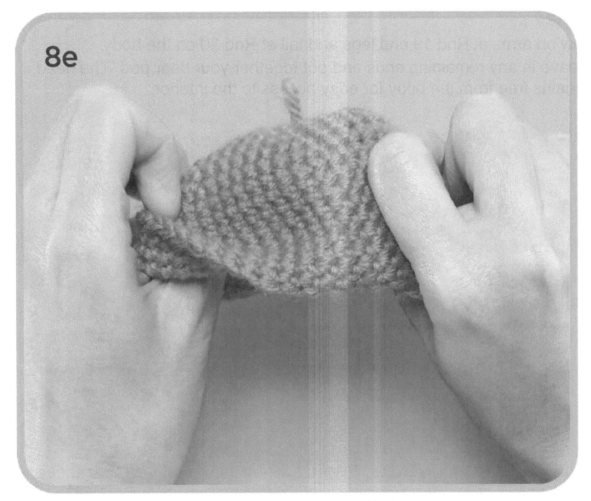

Rnd 18: *2sc in next st, 11sc* in back loops only (52)

Rnd 19: 1sc in each stitch in back loops only (52)

Rnd 20: 1sc in each stitch

• Change to antique white yarn.

Rnd 21–26: 1sc in each stitch. (52)

• Change to light blue yarn.

Rnd 27: 1sc in each stitch (52)

Rnd 28: *sc2tog, 11sc* (48)

Rnd 29: *sc2tog, 6sc* (42)

Rnd 30: *sc2tog, 5sc* (36)

Rnd 31: *sc2tog, 4sc* (30)

Rnd 32: *sc2tog, 3sc* (24)

Rnd 33: *sc2tog, 2sc* (18)

Rnd 34: *sc2tog, 1sc* (12)

Rnd 35: sc2tog around ring (6)

• Close with sl st and weave in ends. Fold the inner (solid green) portion inside the striped half, creating a bowl.

FINISHING:

- Sew on arms at Rnd 19 and legs and tail at Rnd 30 on the body.
- Weave in any remaining ends and put together your bear pod. The head remains free from the body for easy access to the interior.

dog

FROM TERI CREWS IN ILLINOIS

Teri owns two dogs, so it seems fitting that she is contributing an adorable pup. Although he comes with a collar, you don't need to take him on walks—unless you want to. With his chubby body and short legs, this canine cutie is a terrific snuggler, and he doesn't bark! Good dog!

what you'll need:

- G/6 (4.0 mm) crochet hook
- worsted weight yarn in buff, dark brown, black, and blue
- brown safety eyes (12mm)
- black safety nose (21mm)
- white felt
- chenille needle
- stuffing

FINISHED SIZE: About 6 inches tall and 9 inches long

Instructions

HEAD: Buff yarn
Rnd 1: ch2, 6sc in 2nd ch from hook (6)
Rnd 2: 2sc in each stitch (12)
Rnd 3: 1sc in each stitch (12)
Rnd 4: *1sc in next st, 2sc in next st* (18)
Rnds 5–7: 1sc in each st (18)
Rnd 8: (1sc) 6x, (hdc) 6x, (1sc) 6x (18)
Rnd 9: *(1sc) 2x, 2sc in next st* (24)
- Stop and attach the safety nose at the very end of the snout. **(fig. 9a)**

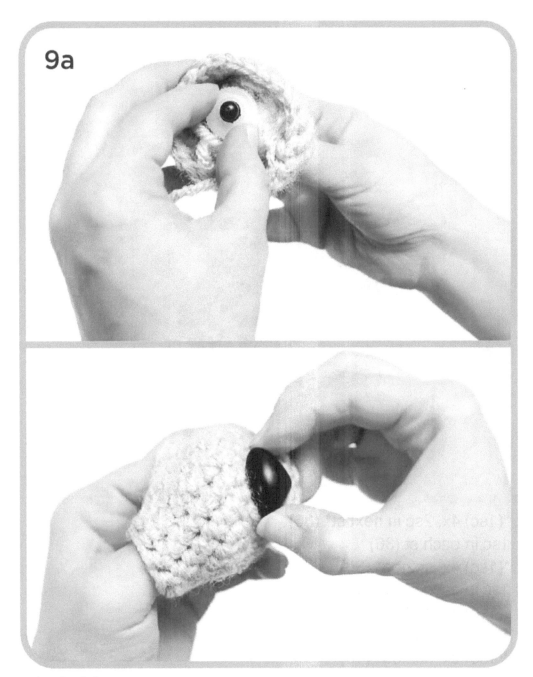

- Change to dark brown yarn.

Rnd 10: 1sc in each st (24)

Rnd 11: *(1sc) 3x, 2sc in next st*(30)

Rnds 12–13: (1sc) 12x, (hdc) 6x, (1sc) 12x (30) **(fig. 9b)**

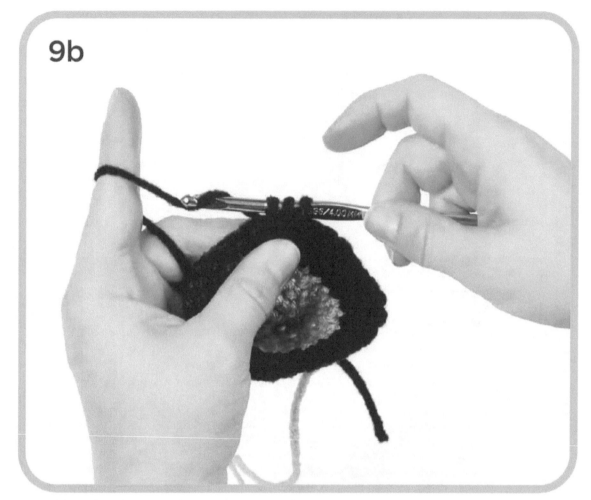

Rnd 14: *(1sc) 4x, 2sc in next st* (36)

Rnd 15: 1sc in each st (36)

Rnd 16: *(1sc) 4x, sc2tog* (30)

Rnd 17: 1sc in each st (30)

Rnd 18: *(1sc) 3x, sc2tog* (24)

Rnd 19: 1sc in each st (24)

Rnd 20: *(1sc) 2x, sc2tog* (18)

Rnd 21: 1sc in each st (18)

• For the eyes, cut two small ovals of white felt using the template shown here. Cut a small slit near the narrow end of each oval and insert the stem of a safety eye. Stuff the head (leaving open) and position the eyes where the snout meets the head. Adjust the felt as desired. Remove the stuffing and secure the eyes.

Rnd 22: *sc2tog* (9)

• Stuff and close, leaving a long tail for sewing.

BODY: Dark brown yarn

Rnd 1: ch2, 6sc in 2nd ch from hook (6)
Rnd 2: 2sc in each stitch (12)
Rnd 3: *1sc, 2sc in next st* (18)
Rnd 4: *(1sc) 2x, 2sc in next st* (24)
Rnd 5: *(1sc) 3x, 2sc in next st* (30)
Rnd 6: *(1sc) 4x, 2sc in next st* (36)
Rnds 7–12: 1sc in each st (36)
Rnd 13: *(1sc) 4x, sc2tog* (30)
Rnds 14–19: 1sc in each st (30)
Rnd 20: *(1sc) 3x, sc2tog* (24)
Rnd 21: *(1sc) 2x, sc2tog* (18)
Rnd 22: *1sc, sc2tog* (12)
• Join with sl st and leave a tail for sewing.
• Stuff and close.

NECK: Dark brown yarn
Rnd 1: ch2, 6sc in 2nd ch from hook (6)
Rnd 2: 2sc in each stitch (12)
Rnds 3–4: 1sc in each st (12)
• Join with sl st and leave a tail for sewing.
• Stuff and close.

EARS (MAKE 2): Dark brown yarn
Rnd 1: ch2, 8sc in 2nd ch from hook (8)
Rnd 2: 2sc in each st (16)
Rnd 3: *1sc, 2sc in next st* (24)
Rnds 4–5: 1sc in each st (24)
Rnd 6: *1sc, sc2tog* (16) **(fig. 9c)**

9c

Rnds 7–11: 1sc in each st (16)

Rnd 12: sc2tog, sc in each remaining st (15)

Rnds 13–15: repeat Rnd 12 (12)

Rnd 16: *(sc2tog*) 6x (6)

• Finish off, leaving a long tail for sewing.

• Flatten the ear and use tail yarn to sew closed.

• Sew the ears to the sides of the head.

LEGS (MAKE 4): Buff yarn

Rnd 1: ch2, 6sc in 2nd ch from hook (6)

Rnd 2: (2sc) 6x (12)

• change to dark brown. **(fig. 9e)**

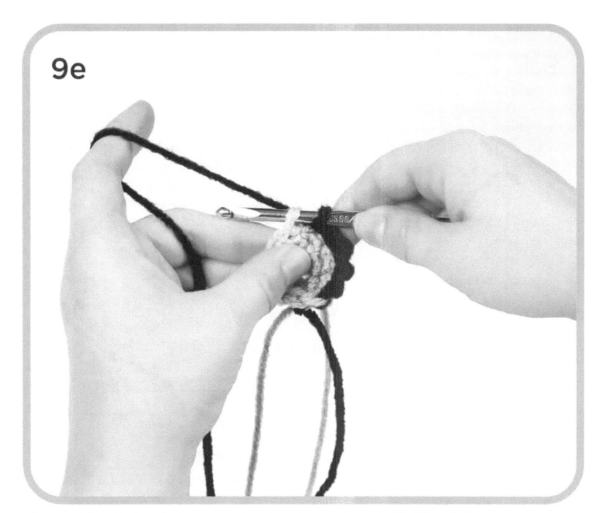

9e

Rnd 3: working in back loops only, 1sc in each st (12) **(fig. 9d)**

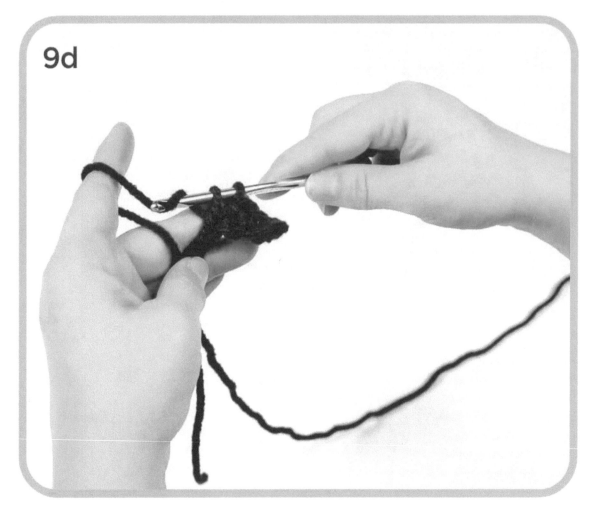

9d

Rnds 4–6: 1sc in each st (12)

Rnd 7: sc2tog, sc in each remaining st (11)

Rnd 8: repeat Rnd 7 (10)

Rnds 9–10: 1sc in each st (10)

Rnd 11: (sc2tog) 2x, sc in each remaining st (8)

• Join with sl st and leave a tail.

• Stuff and close.

TAIL: Dark brown yarn

• Working in rows:

Row 1: ch 7, 1sc in 2nd ch from hook and each ch (6), turn

Row 2: ch 1, 1sc in each 1sc (6), turn

Rows 3–7: repeat Rnd 2, turn

Row 8: ch 1, skip first st, (1sc) 2x, skip next st, sc in last 2 sts (4), turn

Row 9: ch 1, 1sc in each st (4), turn

Rows 10–12: repeat Rnd 9 (4), turn, change to buff yarn.

Rows 13–14: repeat Rnd 9 (4), turn

Row 15: ch 1, (skip next st, sc in next st) 2x (2), turn
Rows 16–18: ch 1sc in each st, turning at end of each row. (2)
• Fold tail in half with wrong sides together, then stuff while sewing tail closed.

COLLAR: Blue yarn
• Working in a row:
Row 1: ch 15, dc in 3rd ch from hook and each ch (12)

FINISHING:
1. Add a small mouth using two plies of yarn.
2. Sew the neck to the top front of the body.
3. Sew the head to the neck.
4. Attach the legs about halfway between the bottom and top of the body.
5. Wrap the collar around the pup's neck and sew the ends together.

alpaca

FROM AERON AANSTOOS IN AUSTIN, TEXAS

Aeron's specialty is sea creatures, but she made this adorable alpaca just for us. It seemed appropriate to include an alpaca in this guide, as they are significant providers of wool. But please don't shear this little guy—he's only for cuddling and loving. You'll enjoy making these so much that soon you'll have your own herd!

what you'll need:

• E/4 (3.5 mm) crochet hook

- **bulky weight acrylic yarn in white and gray**
- **black safety eyes (6 mm)**
- **gray embroidery floss**
- **chenille needle**
- **embroidery needle**
- **stuffing**
- **slicker brush (optional)**

FINISHED SIZE: About 7 inches tall

Instructions

NECK: White yarn
- Make adjustable ring.
Rnd 1: 6sc into ring (6)
Rnd 2: 2sc in each stitch (12)
Rnd 3: *(1sc) 3x, 2sc in next stitch* (15)
Rnds 4–14: 1sc in each stitch (15)
Rnd 15: *1sc, (2sc in next stitch) 2x* (25)
- Close with sl st, leaving a tail for sewing.

BODY: White yarn
- Make adjustable ring.
Rnd 1: 5sc in ring (5)
Rnd 2: 2sc in each stitch (10)
Rnd 3: *1sc, 2sc in next stitch* (15)
Rnd 4: *(1sc) 2x, 2sc in next stitch* (20)
Rnd 5: *(1sc) 3x, 2sc in next stitch* (25)
Rnds 6–18: 1sc in each stitch (25)
Rnd 19: *(1sc) 3x, sc2tog* (20)
Rnd 20: *(1sc) 2x, sc2tog* (15)
- Begin stuffing.
Rnd 21: *1sc, sc2tog* (10) **(fig. 10a)**

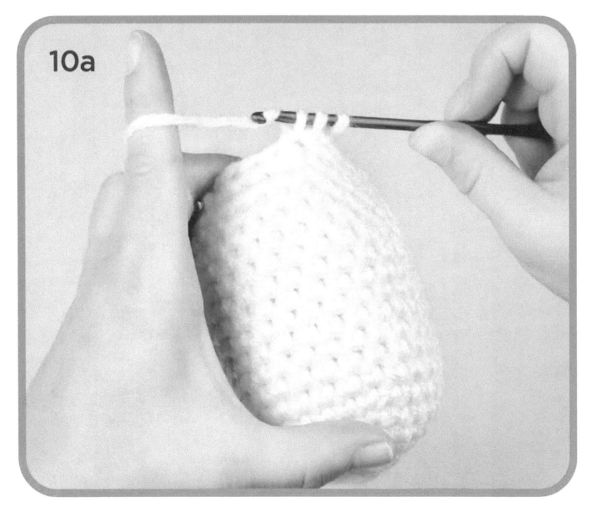

10a

• Finish stuffing firmly.

Rnd 22: *(sc2tog*) 5x (5)

• Close with sl st. Weave in yarn tail, making sure the last round is closed tightly.

LEGS (MAKE 4): Start with gray yarn

• Make adjustable ring.

Rnd 1: 6sc in ring (6)

Rnd 2: *(1sc) 2x, 2sc in next stitch* (8)

Rnd 3: 1sc in each stitch (8)

• Change to white yarn.

Rnd 4: sl st in each stitch in front loops only (8) **(fig. 10b)**

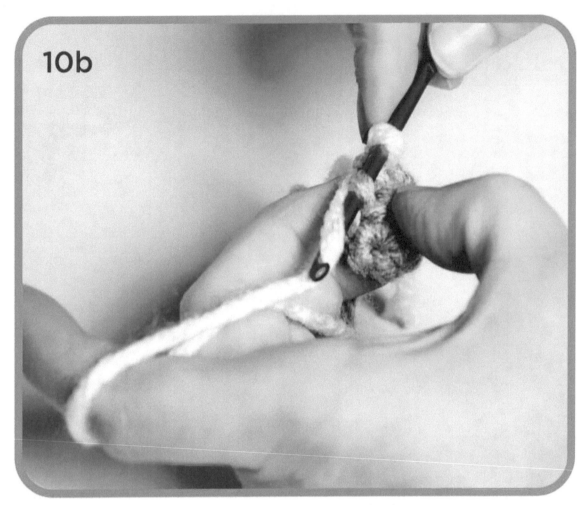

Rnd 5: *1sc, 2sc in next stitch* in front loops only (12)

Rnds 6–9: 1sc in each stitch (12)

Rnd 10: (2sc in next stitch) 5x (10)

- This is an incomplete round. Finish with sl st in the next stitch, leaving a tail for sewing. **(fig. 10c)**

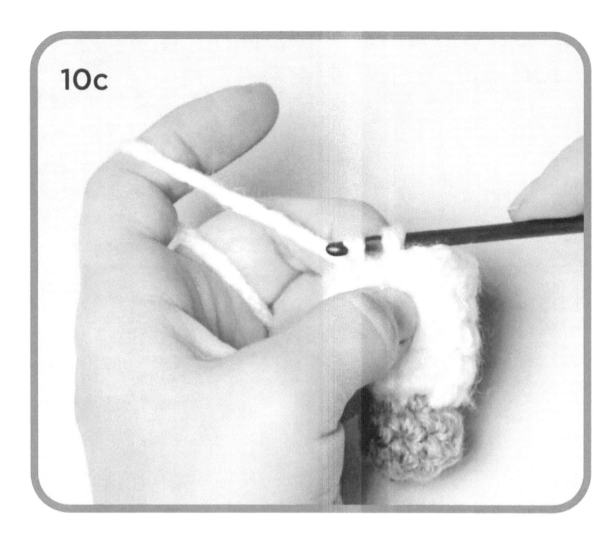

FACE: White yarn

• Make adjustable ring.

Rnd 1: 6sc in ring (6)

Rnd 2: 1sc in each stitch (6)

Rnd 3: *(1sc) 2x, 2sc in next stitch* (8)

Rnds 4–5: 1sc in each stitch (8)

Rnd 6: 1sc, 2sc in next stitch, 1sc, (2sc in next stitch) 2x, 1sc, 2sc in next stitch, 1sc (12)

• Close with sl st, leaving a tail for sewing.

EARS (MAKE 2): White yarn

• Ch 6. Sl st in second chain from hook, hdc in next stitch, 2dc, sl sl in last stitch. (5) **(fig. 10d)**

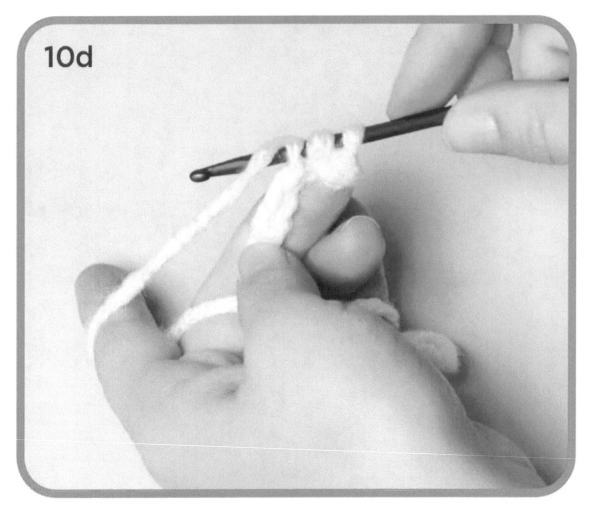

10d

• Finish off, leaving a long tail for sewing.

TAIL: White yarn
• Make adjustable ring.
Rnd 1: 5sc in ring (5)
Rnd 2: 1sc in each stitch (5)
Rnd 3: 2sc in next stitch, (1sc) 4x (6)
Rnd 4: 2sc in next stitch, (1sc) 5x (7)
Rnd 5: (2sc in next stitch) 3x (6)
• This is an incomplete round. Finish with sl st, leaving a tail for sewing.

FINISHING:
1. Cut six lengths of white yarn, each about 6 inches long. Knot all six strands and tie together at one end. Use a chenille needle to pull the long ends of the yarn through the top of the neckpiece between Rnds 1 and 2, catching the knot on the inside. **(fig. 10e)**

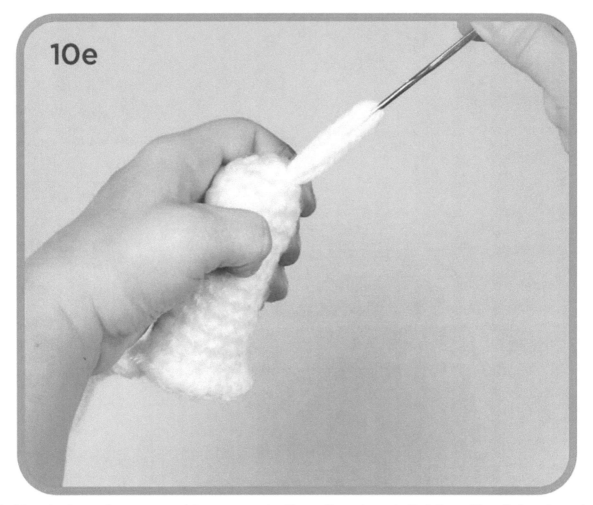

10e

2. Unwind each yarn end to separate the plies, brush lightly with slicker brush, and trim to desired length to create the tuft of hair on top of the alpaca's head.

3. Stuff neck.

4. Fasten the safety eyes on either side of the face, between rows 5 and 6.

5. Sew the face onto the neck.

6. Using six strands of embroidery floss and a sewing needle, embroider the mouth and nose. Stitch over the nose shape three times to make it thicker. **(fig. 10f)**

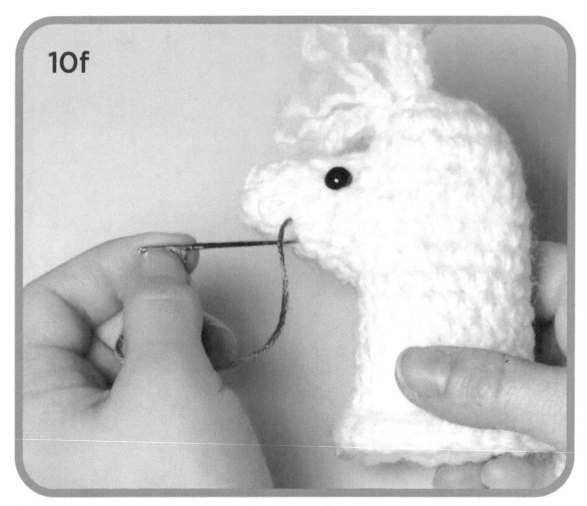

7. Sew the ears to the neck, just above the face.

8. Brush each piece (except for the face and gray hooves) lightly with the slicker brush for a fluffier look (optional).

9. Stuff the legs.

10. Sew the legs to the bottom of the body. The last, incomplete row created a higher edge on the top of each leg. This edge faces the outer corner of the body when the four legs are aligned. **(fig. 10g)**

11. Sew the neck onto the body, making sure it is centered with respect to the front legs.

12. Sew the tail to the back end. The higher-edge side of the last round should face up.

peter pilot duck

FROM KATJA HEINLEIN IN RADEVORMWALD, GERMANY

Katja first found a crochet hook and yarn in her hands when she was eight years old. Her designs have developed from doll's dresses to amigurumi animals, robots, and even aliens! Whether waddling or wading, this adorable duck has quirky personality to spare.

what you'll need:

- C/2 (2.75 mm) crochet hook
- worsted weight cotton yarn in orange and white
- one pair wiggle eyes
- chenille needle
- stuffing

FINISHED SIZE: About 8$^1/_2$ inches tall

Instructions

HEAD AND BODY: White yarn
- Make an adjustable ring.
Rnd 1: 6sc in ring (6)
Rnd 2: 2sc in each sc around (12)
Rnd 3: *1sc, 2sc in next sc* (18)
Rnd 4: *(1sc) 2x, 2sc in next sc* (24)
Rnd 5: *(1sc) 3x, 2sc in next sc* (30)
Rnd 6: Work 1sc in each stitch (30)
Rnd 7: (1sc) 2x, 2sc in next st, (4sc, 2sc in next st) 5x, (1sc) 2x (36) **(fig. 11a)**

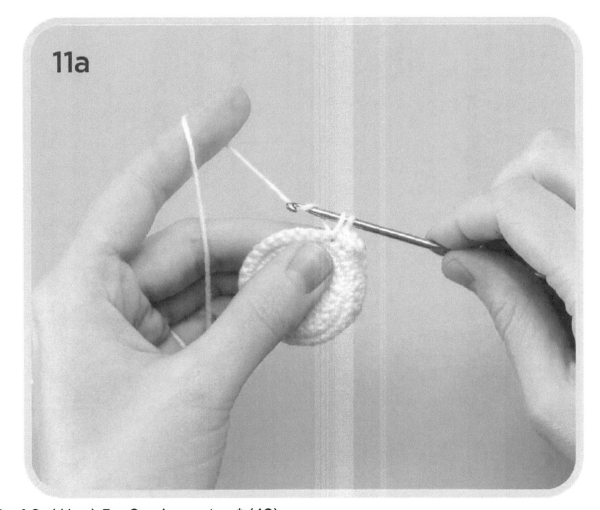

Rnd 8: *(1sc) 5x, 2sc in next sc* (42)

Rnd 9: Work 1sc in each stitch (42)

Rnd 10: (1sc) 3x, 2sc in next st, (6sc, 2sc in next st) 5x, (1sc) 3x (48)

Rnd 11: *(1sc) 7x, 2sc in next st* (54)

Rnd 12-26: 1sc in each stitch (54)

Rnd 27: *(1sc) 7x, sc2tog* (48)

Rnd 28: 1sc in each stitch (48)

Rnd 29: (1sc) 3x, sc2tog (6sc, sc2tog) 5x, (1sc) 3x (42)

Rnd 30: 1sc in each stitch (42)

Rnd 31: sc2tog, (5sc, sc2tog) 5x, (1sc) 5x (36)

Rnd 32: 1sc in each stitch (36)

Rnd 33: (1sc) 2x, sc2tog, (4sc, sc2tog) 5x, (1sc) 2x (30)

• Begin stuffing. **(fig. 11b)**

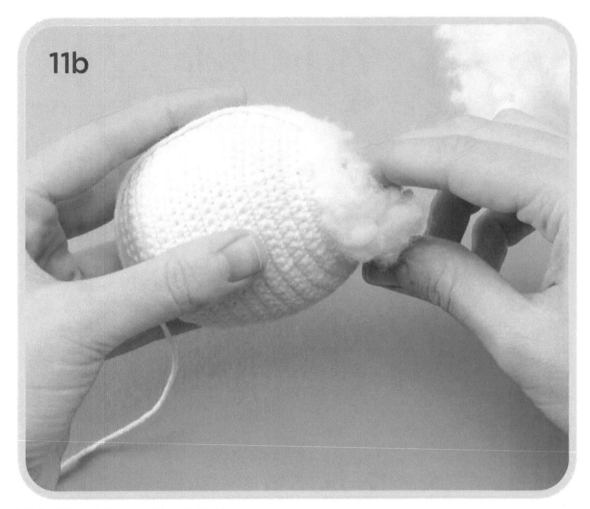

Rnd 34: *(1sc) 3x, sc2tog* (24)

Rnd 35–48: 1sc in each stitch (24)

• Continue stuffing.

Rnd 49: (4, 2sc in next sc) 4x, (1sc) 4x (28)

Rnd 50: 1sc, 2sc in next st, (1sc) 24x, 2sc in next st, 1sc (30)

Rnd 51: 1sc, 2sc in next st, (1sc) 26x, 2sc in next st, 1sc (32)

Rnd 52: 1sc, 2sc in next st, (1sc) 28x, 2sc in next st, 1sc (34)

Rnd 53: 1sc, 2sc in next st, (1sc) 10x, 2sc in next st, (1sc) 8x, 2sc in next st, (1sc) 10x, 2sc in next st, 1sc (38)

Rnd 54: 1sc, 2sc in next st, (1sc) 10x, 2sc in next st, (1sc) 12x, 2sc in next st, (1sc) 10x, 2sc in next st, 1sc (42)

Rnd 55: 1sc, 2sc in next st, (1sc) 13x, 2sc in next st, (1sc) 10x, 2sc in next st, (1sc) 13x, 2sc in next st, 1sc (46)

Rnd 56: 1sc, 2sc in next st, (1sc) 42x, 2sc in next st, 1sc (48)

Rnd 57: 1sc, 2sc in next st, (1sc) 13x, 2sc in next st, (1sc) 2x, 2sc in next st, (1sc) 10x, 2sc in next st, (1sc) 2x, 2sc in next st, (1sc) 13x, 2sc in next st, 1sc (54)

Rnd 58: 1sc, 2sc in next sc, (1sc) 50x, 2sc in next st, 1sc (56)

Rnd 59: 1sc in each stitch (56)

Rnd 60: 1sc, 2sc in next st, (1sc) 18x, 2sc in next st, (1sc) 14x, 2sc in next st, (1sc) 18x, 2sc in next st, 1sc (60)

Rnd 61: 1sc, 2sc in next st, (1sc) 56x, 2sc in next st, 1sc (62)

Rnd 62: 1sc, 2sc in next st, (1sc) 20x, 2sc in next st, (1sc) 16x, 2sc in next st, (1sc) 20x, 2sc in next st, 1sc (66)

Rnd 63–64: 1sc in each stitch (66 sts)

Rnd 65: 1sc, sc2tog, (1sc) 18x, sc2tog, (1sc) 20x, sc2tog, (1sc) 18x, sc2tog, 1sc (62)

Rnd 66: 1sc, sc2tog, (1sc) 56x, sc2tog, 1sc (60)

Rnd 67: 1sc, sc2tog, (1sc) 54x, sc2tog, 1sc (58)

Rnd 68: 1sc, sc2tog, (1sc) 52x, sc2tog, 1sc (56)

Rnd 69: 1sc, sc2tog, (1sc) 50x, sc2tog, 1sc (54)

Rnd 70: *(1sc) 7x, sc2tog* (48) **(fig. 11c)**

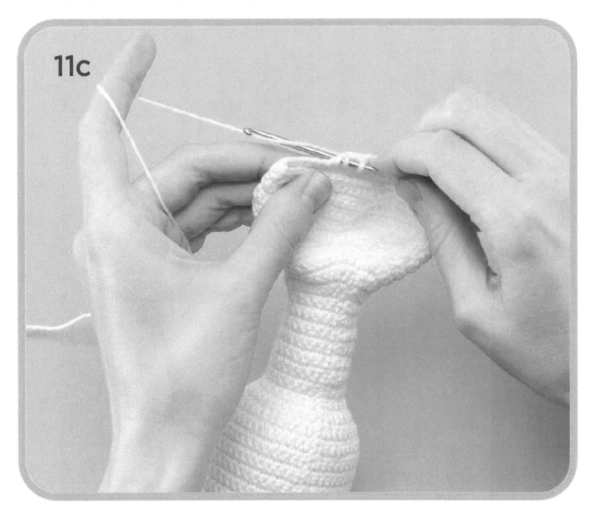

Rnd 71: *(1sc) 6x, sc2tog* (42)

Rnd 72: 1sc in each stitch (42)
Rnd 73: *(1sc) 5x, sc2tog* (36)
Rnd 74: (1sc) 2x, sc2tog, (4sc, sc2tog) 5x, (1sc) 2x (30)
Rnd 75: *(1sc) 3x, sc2tog* (24)
Rnd 76: *(1sc) 2x, sc2tog* (18)
Rnd 77: *1sc, sc2tog* (12)
Rnd 78: *sc2tog* (6 sts)
• Close with a slip knot and weave in the ends.

FEET (MAKE 2): Orange yarn
• Make adjustable ring.
Rnd 1: 6sc in ring (6)

Rnd 2: 2sc in next st, 1sc, (2sc in next st) 2x, 1sc, 2sc in next st (10)

Rnd 3: 2sc in next st, (1sc) 3x, (2sc in next st) 2x, (1sc) 3x, 2sc in next st (14)

Rnd 4: 2sc in next st, (1sc) 5x, (2sc in next st) 2x, (1sc) 5x, 2sc in next st (18)

Rnd 5: 1sc in each stitch (18)

Rnd 6: 2sc in next st, (1sc) 7x, (2sc in next st) 2x, (1sc) 7x, 2sc in next st (22)

Rnd 7: 2sc in next st, (1sc) 9x, (2sc in next st) 2x, (1sc) 9x, 2sc in next st (26)

Rnd 8: 1sc in each stitch (26)

Rnd 9: (1sc) 6x, 3sc in next st, (1sc) 12x, 3sc in next st, (1sc) 6x (30)

Rnd 10: (1sc) 7x, 3sc in next st, (1sc) 14x, 3sc in next st, (1sc) 7x (34)

Rnd 11: 1sc in each stitch (34 sts)

Rnd 12: (1sc) 8x, 3sc in next st, (1sc) 16x, 3sc in next st, (1sc) 8x (38)

Rnd 13: (1sc) 9x, 3sc in next st, (1sc) 18x, 3sc in next st, (1sc) 9x (42)

Rnd 14–15: 1sc in each stitch (42 sts)

Rnd 16: (1sc) 10x, 3sc in next st, (1sc) 20x, 3sc in next st, (1sc) 10x (46)

Rnd 17: (1sc) 11x, 3sc in next st, (1sc) 22x, 3sc in next st, (1sc) 11x (50)

Rnd 18: 1sc in each stitch (50)

Rnd 19: (1sc) 12x, 3sc in next st, (1sc) 24x, 3sc in next st, (1sc) 12x (54)

Rnd 20: (1sc) 13x, 3sc in next st, (1sc) 26x, 3sc in next st, (1sc) 13x (58)

• Close the foot: Join the two sides together with single crochet. **(fig. 11d)**

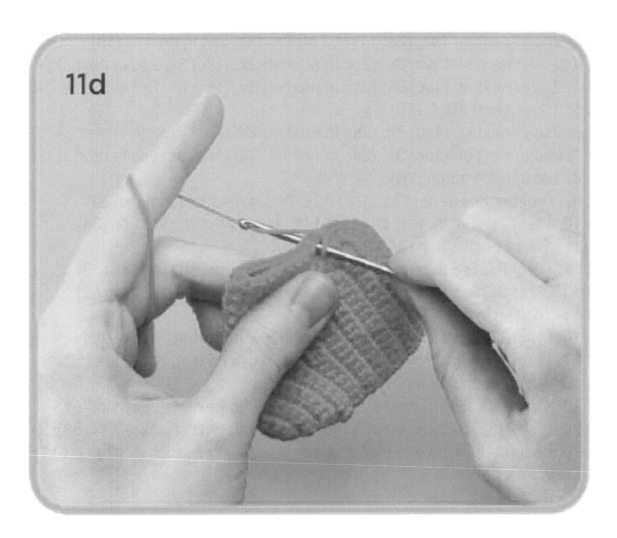

11d

LEGS (MAKE 2): Orange yarn

• Make adjustable ring.

Rnd 1: 6sc in ring (6)

Rnd 2: 2sc in next st, 1sc, (2sc in next st) 2x, 1sc, 2sc in next st (10)

Rnd 3: 2sc in next st, (1sc) 3x, (2sc in next st) 2x, (1sc) 3x, 2sc in next st (14)

Rnd 4–17: 1sc in each stitch (14 sts)

• Stuff each leg and sew closed.

WINGS (MAKE 4): White yarn

• The wings are worked flat, turning work at the end of each row.

Row 1: Ch 2, 2sc in 2nd ch from hook. (2)
Row 2: 2sc in each stitch (4)
Row 3: 2sc in next st, (1sc) 3x (5)
Row 4: 1sc in each stitch (5)
Row 5: 2sc in next st, (1sc) 4x (6)
Row 6: 1sc in each stitch (6)
Row 7: 2sc in next st, (1sc) 5x (7)
Row 8: 1sc in each stitch (7)
Row 9: 2sc in next st, (1sc) 6x (8)
Row 10: 1sc in each stitch (8)
Row 11: 2sc in next st, (1sc) 7x (9)
Row 12: 1sc in each stitch (9)
Row 13: 2sc in next st, (1sc) 8x (10)
Row 14–16: 1sc in each stitch (10)
Row 17: sc2tog, (1sc) 8x (9)
Row 18: sc2tog, (1sc) 5x, sc2tog (7)
Row 19: sc2tog, (1sc) 3x, sc2tog (5)

BILL: Orange yarn

• Make adjustable ring.

Rnd 1: Make 6sc in ring (6)
Rnd 2: *(1sc) 2x, 2sc in next st* (8)
Rnd 3: *(1sc) 3x, 2sc in next st* (10)
Rnd 4: *(1sc) 4x, 2sc in next st* (12)
Rnd 5: *(1sc) 5x, 2sc in next st* (14)
Rnd 6: *(1sc) 6x, 2sc in next st* (16)
Rnd 7: *(1sc) 7x, 2sc in next st* (18)

• Sew closed, then sew the bill on the head.

FINISHING:

1. Hold two wings together. Join the pieces together with single crochet. Repeat for second wing. **(see fig. 11e and 11f)**

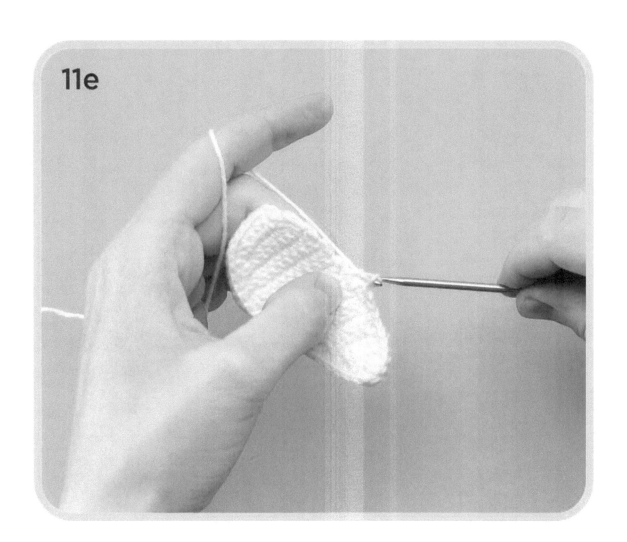

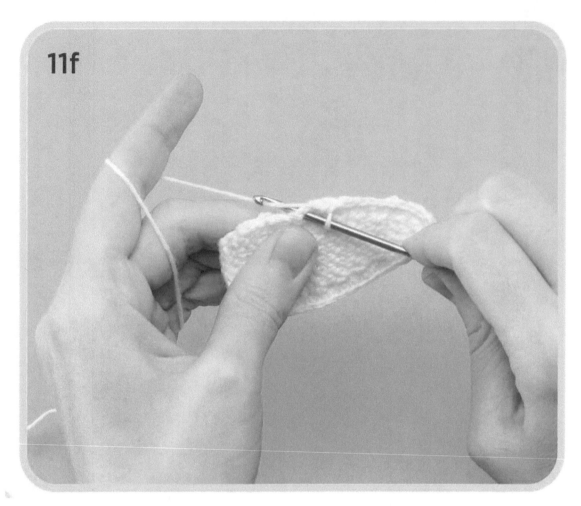

11f

2. Sew wings onto the body.
3. Glue eyes onto the head above the bill.

owl

FROM HEATHER JARMUSZ IN ILLINOIS

Whoooo wouldn't love this adorable owl? While most owls are known to be solitary animals, this one loves company. You'll be addicted to making these adorable, big-eyed creatures!

FINISHED SIZE: About 6 inches tall

Instructions

EYE PATCHES (MAKE 2): White yarn
• Make an adjustable ring.
Rnd 1: 6sc in ring (6)
Rnd 2: 2sc in each st (12)
Rnd 3: *2sc in next st, sc in next st* (18)
Rnd 4: *2sc in next st, 2sc* (24)
• Finish off, leaving a long tail for sewing to face.

HEAD AND BODY: Start with brown yarn
• Make an adjustable ring.
Rnd 1: 6sc in ring (6)
Rnd 2: 2sc in each st (12)
Rnd 3: *2sc in next st, sc in next st* (18)
Rnd 4: *2sc in next st, 2sc* (24)
Rnd 5: *2sc in next st, 3sc* (30)
Rnd 6: *2sc in next st, 4sc* (36)
Rnd 7: *2sc in next st, 5sc* (42)
Rnd 8–20: sc in each st (42)
• Position the eye patches and attach the safety eyes through both layers between rounds 13 and 14. Fasten the safety eyes securely. **(fig. 12a)**

12a

Rnd 21: *invdec over next 2 sts, 5sc* (36) **(fig. 12b)**

Rnd 22: *invdec over next 2 sts, 4sc* (30)

Rnd 23: *invdec over next 2 sts, 3sc* (24)

Rnd 24: *invdec over next 2 sts, 2sc* (18)

• Change to sage yarn.

• Stuff the head firmly.

Rnd 25: sc in each st (18)

Rnd 26: *2sc in next st, 2sc* (24)

• Change to light green yarn.

Rnd 27: *2sc in next st, 3sc* (30)

Rnd 28: 1sc in each st (30)

• Change to sage yarn.

Rnd 29–30: 1sc in each st (30)

• Change to light green yarn. **(fig. 12c)**

Rnd 31–32: 1sc in each st (30)

• Change to sage yarn.

Rnd 33–34: 1sc in each st (30)

• Change to light green yarn.

Rnd 35–36: sc in each st (30)

• Change to sage yarn.

Rnd 37–38: sc in each st (30)

• Change to light green yarn.

Rnd 39: *invdec over next 2 sts, 3sc* (24)

Rnd 40: *invdec over next 2 sts, 2sc* (18)

• Change to sage yarn.

Rnd 41: *invdec over next 2 sts, sc in next st* (12)

• Stuff the body firmly. **(see fig. 12d)**

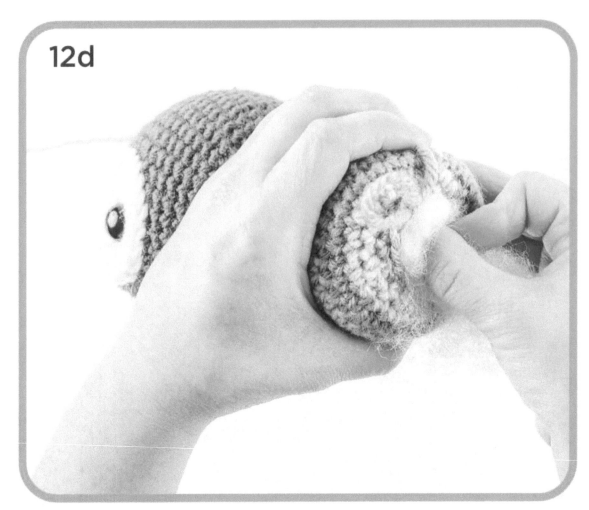

Rnd 42: invdec around (6)

• Finish off, closing up the hole.

• Weave in the ends.

EARS (MAKE 2): Brown yarn

• Make an adjustable ring.

Rnd 1: 4sc in ring (4)

Rnd 2: *2sc in next st, sc in next st* (6)

Rnd 3: *2sc in next st, 2sc* (8)

Rnd 4: *2sc in next st, 3sc* (10)

Rnd 5: *2sc in next st, 4sc* (12)

• Finish off, leaving a long tail for sewing.

• Sew the ear closed **(see fig. 12e)**, then sew it to the top edge of the head.

12e

BEAK: Orange yarn
• Make an adjustable ring.
Rnd 1: 4sc in ring (4)
Rnd 2: *2sc in next st, sc in next st* (6)
Rnd 3: *2sc in next st, 2sc* (8)
Rnd 4: *2sc in next st, 3sc* (10)
• Finish off, leaving a long tail for sewing. Stuff lightly and sew to the face.

FEET (MAKE 2): Orange yarn
• Make an adjustable ring.
Rnd 1: 6sc in ring (6 sts).
Rnd 2: 2sc in each st (12)
Rnd 3: 1sc in each st (12)
Rnd 4: *invdec over next 2 sts, sc in next st* (8)
• Finish off, leaving a long tail for sewing.
• Sew the foot closed, then sew it to the front of body. **(fig. 12f)**

• Weave in ends.

WINGS (MAKE 2): Brown yarn
• Make an adjustable ring.
Rnd 1: 6sc in ring (6)
Rnd 2: 1sc in each st (6)
Rnd 3: *2 sc in next st, sc in next * around (9) **(fig. 12g)**
Rnd 4: sc in each st (9 sts)
Rnd 5: *2 sc in next st, 2sc* (12)
Rnd 6: *2 sc in next st, 3sc* (15)
Rnd 7: *2 sc in next st, 4sc* (18)
Rnd 8: *2 sc in next st, 5sc* (21)
Rnd 9–14: 1sc in each st (21)
Rnd 15: *invdec over next 2 sts, 5sc* (18)
Rnd 16: *invdec over next 2 sts, 4sc* (15)
• Finish off, leaving a long tail for sewing.

• Sew each wing closed, then sew to either side of the body at round 24.

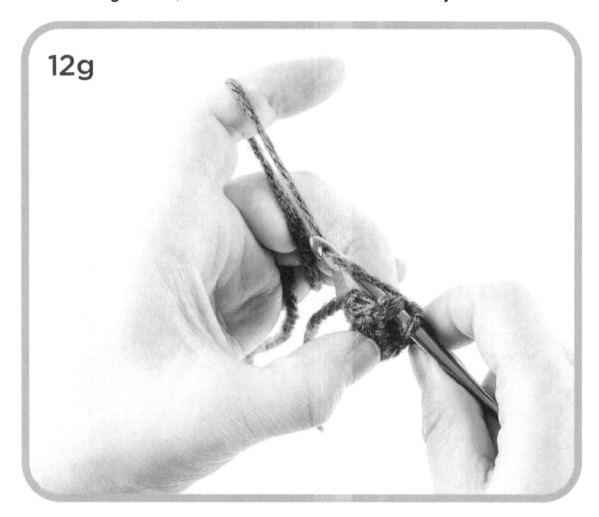

12g

bunny

FROM M. BRIDGES IN STUARTS DRAFT, VIRGINIA

With its pink nose and fluffy tail, this rabbit will bunny hop straight into your heart. You can add your own twist with minor changes in color and details. This little cutie was approved by M.'s own little house bunny, Duncan. You can't get much better than that!

what you'll need:

• G/6 (4.0 mm) crochet hook

- **worsted weight acrylic yarn in tan and white**
- **pink embroidery floss**
- **black safety eyes (6 mm)**
- **pink felt**
- **chenille needle**
- **embroidery needle**
- **stuffing**

FINISHED SIZE: About 5$^1/_2$ inches tall

Instructions

HEAD: Tan yarn
- Make an adjustable ring.

Rnd 1: 6sc in ring
Rnd 2: 2sc in each stitch (12)
Rnd 3: *2sc in next st, 1sc* (18)
Rnd 4: *2sc in next st, (1sc, 2x)* (24)
Rnd 5: *2sc in next st, 3sc* (30)
Rnd 6: *2sc in next st, 4sc* (36)
Rnd 7: *2sc in next st, 5sc* (42)
Rnds 8–13: 1sc in each stitch (42)
Rnd 14: *sc2tog, 5sc* (36) **(fig. 13a)**

13a

Rnd 15: *sc2tog, 4sc* (30)
Rnd 16: *sc2tog, 3sc* (24)
Rnd 17: *sc2tog, 2sc (18)
• Stuff.
• Attach the safety eyes and stitch a nose using pink embroidery floss. **(fig. 13b)**

Rnd 18: *sc2tog, 1sc* (12)
Rnd 19: *sc2tog* (6)

BODY: Tan yarn
• Make an adjustable ring.
Rnd 1: 6sc in ring
Rnd 2: 2sc in each stitch (12)
Rnd 3: *2sc in next st, 1sc* (18)
Rnd 4: *2sc in next st, 2sc* (24)
Rnd 5: *2sc in next st, 3 sc* (30)
Rnd 6: *2sc in next st, 4 sc* (36)
Rnds 7–9: 1 sc in each stitch (36)
Rnd 10: *sc2tog, 4sc* (30)
Rnd 11: 1 sc in each stitch (30)
Rnd 12: *sc2tog, 3sc* (24)
Rnd 13: 1 sc in each stitch (24)
Rnd 14: *sc2tog, 2sc (18)

• Stuff.
Rnd 15: *sc2tog, 1sc* (12)
Rnd 16: *sc2tog* (6)
• Finish off, leaving a long tail for sewing.

EARS (MAKE 2): Tan yarn
• Make an adjustable ring.
Rnd 1: 6sc in ring
Rnd 2: 2sc in each stitch (12)
Rnd 3: *2sc in next st, 1sc* (18)
Rnds 4–5: 1sc in each stitch (18)
Rnd 6: *sc2tog, 1sc (12)
Rnds 7–9: 1sc in each stitch (12) **(fig. 13c)**

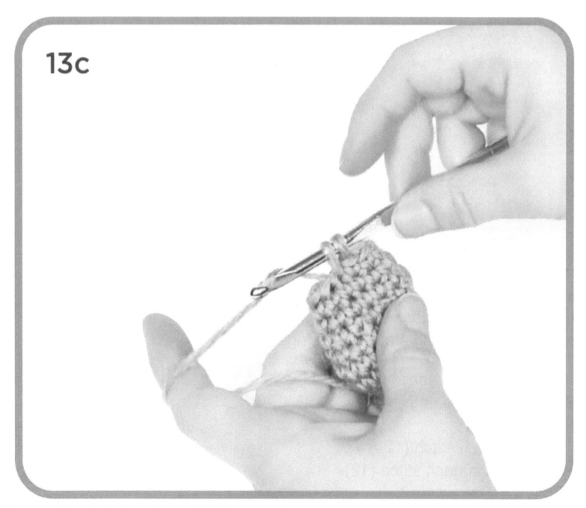

13c

• Close with sl st, leaving a tail for sewing.

ARMS (MAKE 2): Tan yarn
• Make an adjustable ring.

Rnd 1: 6sc in ring
Rnd 2: *2sc in next st, 1sc, 2sc in next st* (10) **(fig. 13d)**

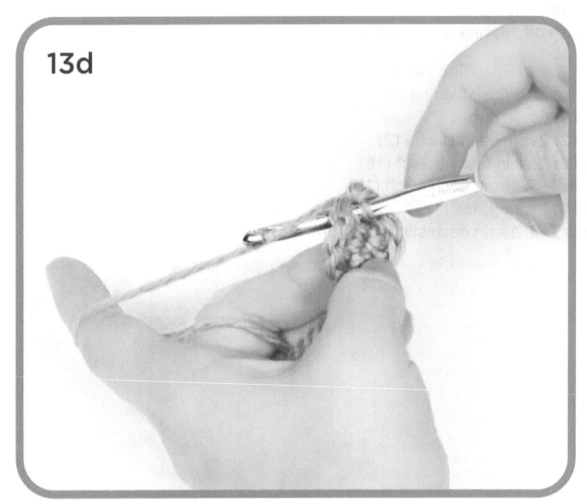

13d

Rnds 3–5: 1 sc in each stitch (10)
• Stuff the arm.
Rnd 6: *sc2tog, 1sc, sc2tog* (6)
• Close with sl st, leaving a tail for sewing.

FEET (MAKE 2): Tan yarn
• Make an adjustable ring.
Rnd 1: 6sc in ring
Rnd 2: 2sc in each stitch (12)
Rnds 3–8: 1 sc in each stitch (12)
• Stuff the foot.
Rnd 9: *sc2tog* (6) **(fig. 13e)**

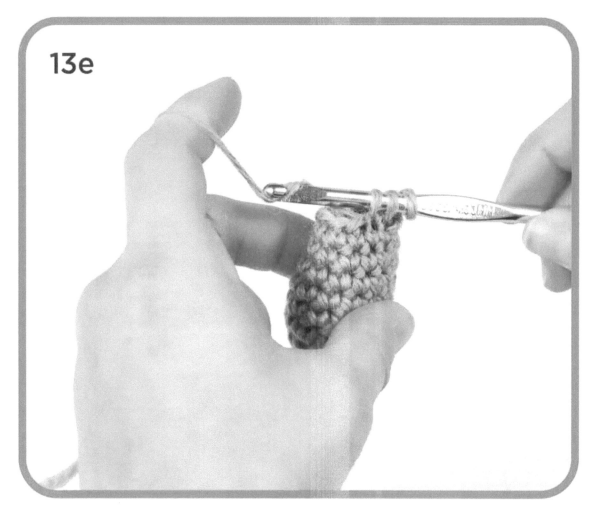

13e

- Close with sl st, leaving a tail for sewing.

TAIL: White yarn
- Cut a $1^1/_2$" x $2^3/_4$" piece of thin cardboard (use the pompom template shown here).
- Wrap 3 feet of yarn around the card.
- Slide the yarn off the card and use another piece of yarn to tie the bundle tightly in the middle. **(fig. 13f)**

13f

• Clip each of the loops and shake the pompom to make it fluffy. **(fig. 13g)**

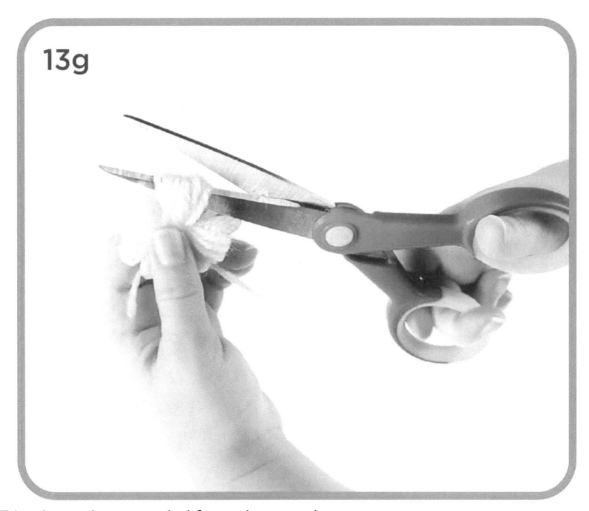

13g

• Trim the ends as needed for a nice round pompom.

FINISHING

1. Stuff the head and body firmly. Sew the head to the body.
2. Using the template shown here, cut pink felt to fit inside the ears. Using a single strand of embroidery floss, stitch the felt into the ears.
3. Sew the ears to the head.
4. Sew the arms to the side of the body.
5. Sew the feet to the base so they sit long and flat.
6. Sew the pompom tail to the body.

beaver

FROM BRIGITTE READ IN GLASGOW, SCOTLAND

Brigitte's amigurumi creations are all cute and creative, and this goofy, grinning beaver is no exception. This one even has individual fingers and toes! Slightly fuzzy brown yarn gives the beaver an irresistibly furry coat, and felt adornments bring its signature tail and toothy smile to life!

what you'll need:

- C/2 (2.75 mm) crochet hook
- worsted weight acrylic yarn in brown
- black embroidery floss
- brown and white felt
- black plastic eyes (8 mm)
- chenille needle
- stuffing

FINISHED SIZE: About 5 inches tall

Instructions

BODY: Brown yarn
• Make an adjustable ring.
Rnd 1: 8sc in ring
Rnd 2: 1sc in each stitch (8) **(fig. 14a and 14b)**

14a

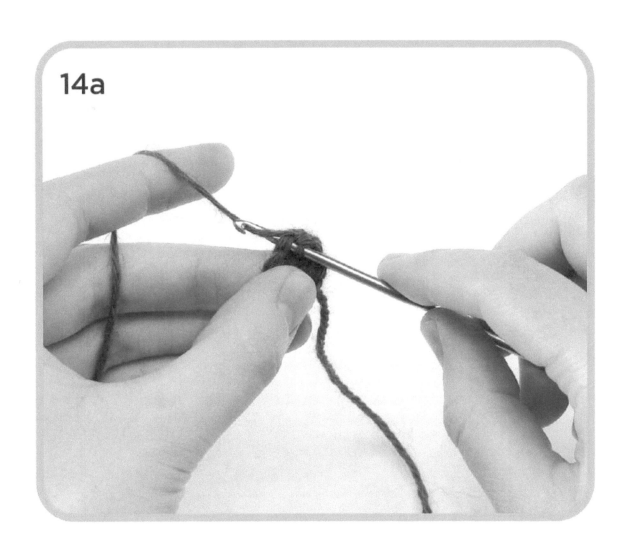

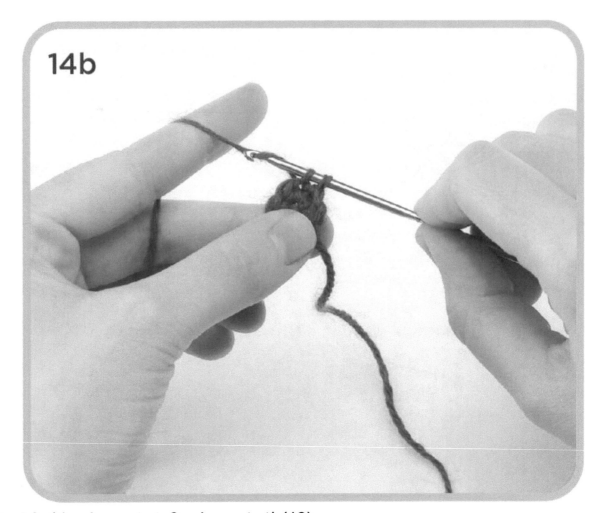

Rnd 3: *1sc in next st, 2sc in next st* (12)
Rnd 4: *(1sc) 2x, 2sc in next st* (16)
Rnd 5: 1sc in each stitch (16)
Rnd 6: *(1sc) 3x, 2sc in next st* (20)
Rnd 7: 1sc in each stitch (20)
Rnd 8: *(1sc) 3x, 2sc in next st* (25)
Rnd 9: 1sc in each stitch (25)
Rnd 10: *(1sc) 4x, 2sc in next st* (30)
Rnd 11–12: 1sc in each stitch (30)
Rnd 13: *(1sc) 5x, 2sc in next st* (35)
Rnd 14–15: 1sc in each stitch (35)
Rnd 16: *(1sc) 6x, 2sc in next st* (40)
Rnd 17–18: 1sc in each stitch (40)
Rnd 19: *(1sc) 7x, 2sc in next st* (45)
Rnd 20–21: 1sc in each stitch (45)
Rnd 22: *(1sc) 8x, 2sc in next st* (50)
Rnd 23–33: 1sc in each stitch (50)

• Close with sl st.

ARMS AND LEGS (MAKE 4): Brown yarn
• Ch4 to make arm. To make each of the three fingers, sl st into the final stitch on the arm, ch4, secure with sl st (making a small loop), and 1sc in each of the remaining three stitches on the finger. Do this two more times to make a total of three fingers. Finish arm by making 1sc in each of the remaining three stitches on the arm.

BASE OF BODY: Brown yarn
• Make an adjustable ring.
Rnd 1: 8sc in ring
Rnd 2: 2sc in each stitch (16)
Rnd 3: *1sc, 2sc in next st* (24) **(fig. 14c)**

Rnd 4: *(1sc) 2x, 2sc in next st* (32)
Rnd 5: *(1sc) 3x, 2sc in next st* (40)
Rnd 6: *(1sc) 4x, 2sc in next st* (48)

Rnd 7: *(1sc) 5x, 2sc in next st* (56)
• Close with sl st.

TAIL: Brown felt
• Cut two tail shapes from felt using the template shown here, sew together with needle and thread, and stuff. **(fig. 14d)**

EARS (MAKE 2): Brown yarn
• Ch4 and sew the ends to the head, creating a curve.

FINISHING:
1. Weave in all ends.
2. Fasten safety eyes above the nose.
3. Stuff body.
4. Align the base with the body and sew together with brown yarn.
5. Sew the tail onto the back edge of the body base.

6. Sew on the arms to the side of the body and the legs to the bottom of the base. **(fig. 14e)**

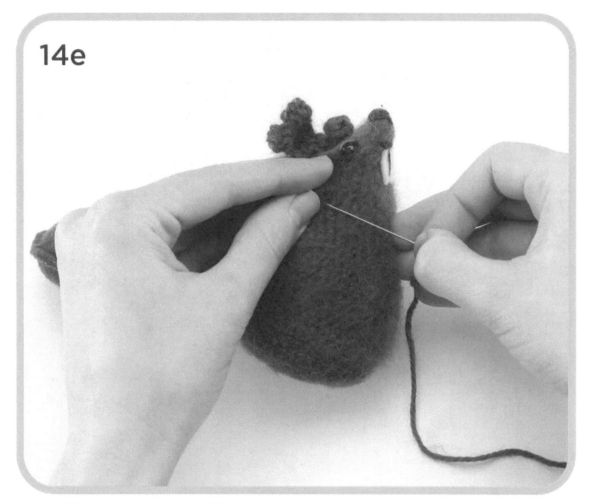

7. Embroider on the nose with black thread.

8. Sew on a small square scrap of white felt for teeth. Use black embroidery floss to sew on a mouth and tooth details.

bear

FROM VICTORIA RODRIGUEZ IN TEXAS

You won't be able to *bear* how cute this little one is! Make these as gifts for friends who could use a bear hug from time to time. You'll be spreading love around town in no time!

what you'll need:

- **F/5 crochet hook**
- **worsted weight acrylic yarn in brown**

- **embroidery floss or thin black yarn**
- **white felt**
- **black safety eyes (10 mm)**
- **black safety nose**
- **chenille needle**
- **embroidery needle**
- **stuffing**

FINISHED SIZE: Approx. $3^1/_2$ inches tall

Instructions

HEAD:
- Make an adjustable ring.

Rnd 1: 6sc into ring (6)

Rnd 2: 2sc in each stitch (12) **(fig. 15a)**

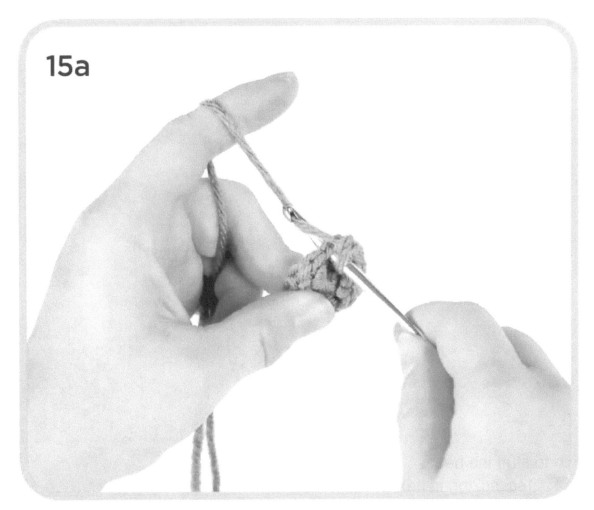

15a

Rnd 3: *1sc, 2sc in next stitch* (18)
Rnd 4: *2sc, 2sc in next stitch* (24)
Rnd 5: *3sc, 2sc in next stitch* (30)
Rnd 6: *4sc, 2sc in next stitch* (36)
Rnd 7-10: 1sc in each stitch (36)
Rnd 11: *4sc, sc2tog* (30)
• Attach eyes between rows 9 and 10.
Rnd 12: *3sc, sc2tog* (24)
Rnd 13: *2sc, sc2tog* (18)
• Cut a 1-inch diameter circle from white felt and stitch on a smile using black embroidery floss or yarn. Cut a small hole above the smile and poke the stem of your safety nose through it. Position the felt piece on the head with the nose between and slightly below the eyes. Stick the nose stem through to the inside and attach the safety backing. **(fig. 15b)**

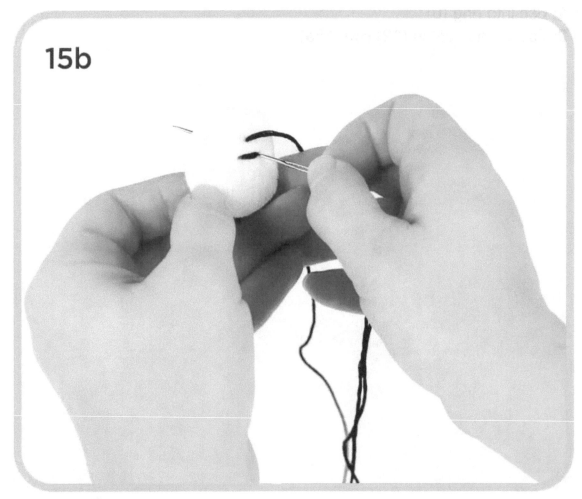

15b

• Begin to stuff the head.
Rnd 14: *1sc, sc2tog in next stitch* (12)

Rnd 15: sc2tog around (6)
• Close.

BODY:
• Make an adjustable ring.
Rnd 1: 6sc into ring (6)
Rnd 2: 2sc in each stitch (12) **(fig. 15c)**

Rnd 3: *1sc, 2sc in next stitch* (18)
Rnd 4: *2sc, 2sc in next stitch* (24)
Rnds 5–7: 1sc in each stitch (24)
Rnd 8: *2sc, sc2tog* (18)
• Stuff and sew to the head.

EARS (MAKE 2):
• Make an adjustable ring.
Rnd 1: 6sc into ring (6)
Rnd 2: 2sc in each stitch (12)

Rnd 3: *1sc, 2sc in next stitch* (18)

Rnds 4–5: 1sc in each stitch (18)

Rnd 6: *1sc, sc2tog* (12)

• Finish off, leaving a long tail for sewing.

• Fold ear in half and use the tail to sew the ear together and onto the head. **(fig. 15d)**

LEGS (MAKE 2):

• Make adjustable ring.

Rnd 1: 6sc into ring (6)

Rnd 2: 2sc in each stitch (12)

Rnds 3–4: 1sc in each stitch (12)

Rnd 5: *2sc, sc2tog in next stitch* (9) **(fig. 15e)**

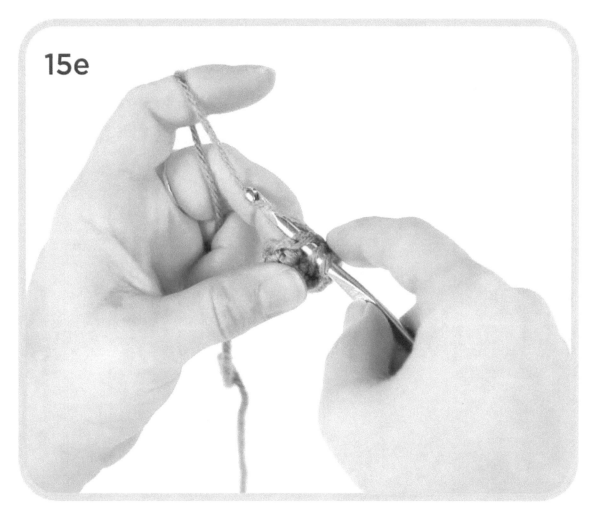

15e

• Stuff and attach to the body.

ARMS (MAKE 2):
• Make an adjustable ring.
Rnd 1: 6sc into ring (6)
Rnd 2: *1sc, 2sc in next stitch* (9)
Rnds 3–6: 1sc in each stitch (9)
• Finish off, leaving a long tail for sewing.
• Stuff and attach to the body.

fish

FROM SANDA JELIC DOBROSAVLJEV IN BOSNIA

A graphic and multimedia designer by day, Sanda turns her eye for sharp design to whimsical patterns with healthy doses of vibrant color. She loves designing projects for children and adults alike. This fish won't fit in a tank, but will still make a splash with your family and friends!

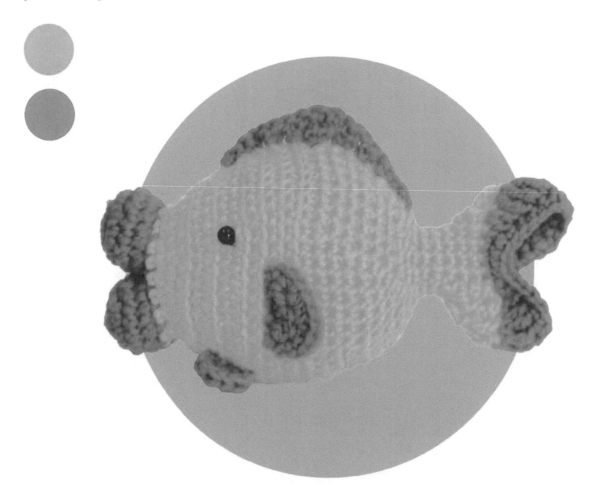

what you'll need:

- C/2 (2.75 mm) crochet hook
- sport weight cotton yarn in red and orange
- black safety eyes (8 mm)

- pins
- chenille needle
- stuffing

FINISHED SIZE: About 5 inches long

Instructions

LIP S AND BODY: Start with red yarn
- Make an adjustable ring.

Rnd 1: 6sc into ring (6)

Rnd 2: 2sc in each stitch (12)

Rnd 3: *1sc, 2sc in next stitch* (18)

- Sl st in next st, cut yarn leaving a 6" tail, and pull yarn through the last loop. This forms the foundation for the top lip.
- Make an adjustable ring.
- Bottom Lip: Red yarn

Rnd 1–3: As rounds 1-2 above.

Rnd 4: 1sc in next 9 stitches

Finishing the top and bottom lips:

1. Insert hook into first stitch after sl st made on top lip and continue to make 1sc in all 18 stitches. Be careful not to miss the last stitch—it's the sl st from the previous row, and it's tiny and easy to miss. (27) **(fig. 16a)**

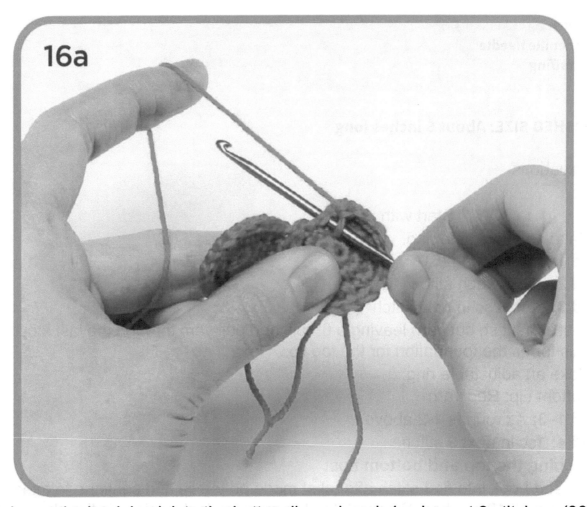

16a

2. Insert the hook back into the bottom lip and work 1sc in next 9 stitches. (36)

3. Use a chenille needle and the tail from the top lip to close the gap between the halves. Leave the tail hanging.

Rnd 5: *sc2tog* (18)

• Change to orange yarn

Rnd 6: 1sc in each stitch (18)

Rnd 7: *(1sc) 2x, 2sc in next stitch* (24)

Rnd 8: *(1sc) 3x, 2sc in next stitch* (30)

Rnd 9: *(1sc) 4x, 2sc in next stitch* (36)

Rnd 10: 1sc in each stitch in back loops only (36)

Rnd 11: *(1sc) 5x, 2sc in next stitch* (42)

Rnd 12: 1sc in each stitch in back loops only (42)

Rnd 13: *(1sc) 6x, 2sc in next stitch* (48)

Rnd 14–17: 1sc in each stitch in back loops only **(fig. 16b)**

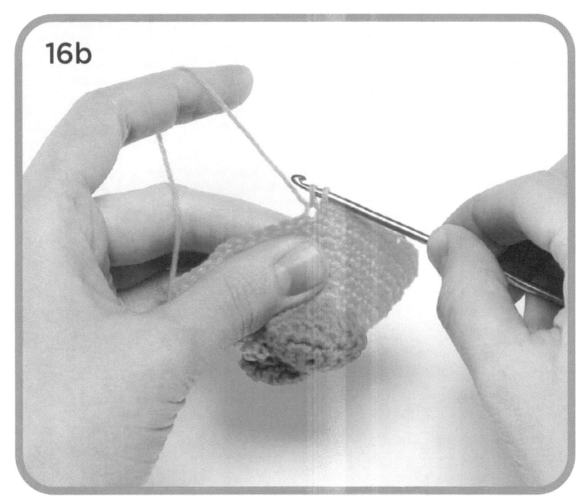

16b

- Begin stuffing, keeping the red yarn tail long and extending past the end of your work.

Rnd 18: *(1sc) 6x, sc2tog* (42)
Rnd 19: 1sc in each stitch (42)
Rnd 20: *(1sc) 5x, sc2tog* (36)
Rnd 21: 1sc in each stitch (36)
Rnd 22: *(1sc) 4x, sc2tog* (30)
Rnd 23: *(1sc) 3x, sc2tog* (24)
Rnd 24: *(1sc) 2x, sc2tog* (18)
- Stuff the body firmly. **(fig. 16c)**

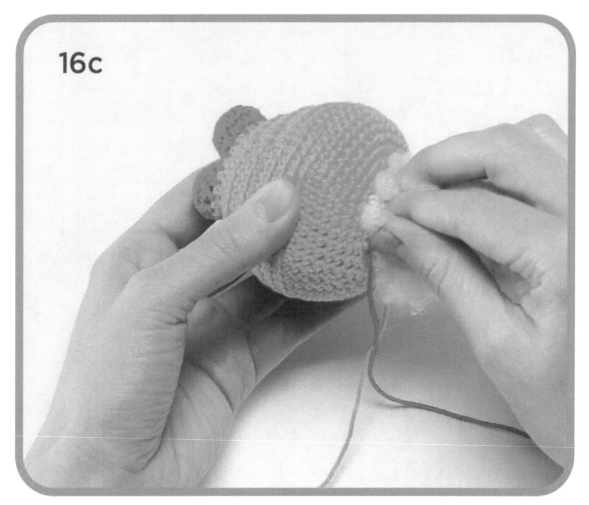

Rnd 25: *1sc, sc2tog* (12)

Rnd 26–28: 1sc around (12)

• Change to orange yarn

Rnd 29: Sc in next 2 sts, dc in next 2 sts, sc in next 4 sts, dc in next 2 sts, sc in next 2 sts (12)

Rnd 30: Sc in next 2 sts, dc and tr in each of next 2 sts, sc in next 4 sts, dc and tr in each of next 2 sts, sc in next 2 sts (16)

Rnd 31: Sc in next 2 sts, dc in next st, 2 tr in next 2 sts, dc in next st, sc in next 4 sts, dc in next st, 2 tr in next 2 sts, dc in next st, sc in next 2 sts (20)

• Change to red in last st.

Rnd 32: 1sc in next 2 sts. 2 dc in next st, 2 tr in next 4 sts, 2 dc in next st, sc in next 4 sts, 2 dc in next st, 2 tr in next 4 sts, 2 dc in next st, sc in next 2 sts (32)

Rnd 33: 1sc around (32)

• Sl st in last stitch. Fasten off and weave in the yarn ends.

TOP FIN: Red yarn

• Attach red yarn to top of fish at round 12.

- Work the following instructions rows, turning the project around and working back on row 2.

Row 1: ch1, sc in same place, 2sc in next row, 2hdc in next row, 2dc in next row, 2tr in next row, 2dc in next row, 2hdc in next row, 2 sc in next row, sc in next 2 rows. Slip st in next row. Turn. **(fig. 16d)**

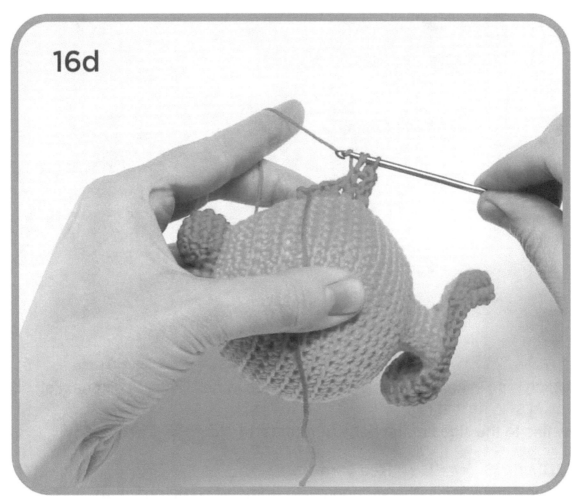

Row 2: 1sc in each st. Sl st in last st and weave in ends.

SIDE FINS (MAKE 2): Red yarn

Rnd 1: ch6, sc, in second chain from hook, hdc, 2dc in next chain, hdc, sc, rotate piece to start next row on the other side of the foundation chain. (6) **(fig. 16e)**

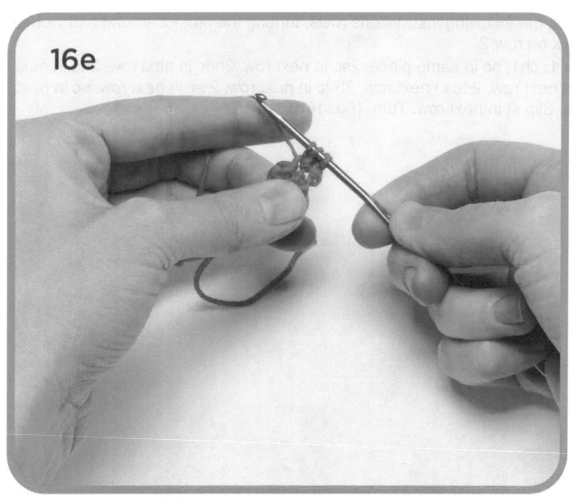

Rnd 2: ch1, sc in next st, 2 sc in next st, 2 hdc in next 2sts, 2sc in next st, sc in next st, sl st in next st (12)
• Sew fins to the sides of the body at rounds 14–15.

BOTTOM FINS (MAKE 2): Red yarn
Rnd 1: ch2, then 3sc in the second chain from the hook. ch1, turn.
Rnd 2: 2 hdc in each of next 2 sts, sl st in last st.
• Sew fins to lower front sides of the body between rounds 11–13.

FINISHING:
1. Attach the eyes about an inch apart between rounds 11 and 12.

hedgehog

FROM AMY GAINES IN SHREWSBURY, MASSACHUSETTS

Amy works out of her home as a freelance crochet designer. From amigurumi animals to purses and accessories, she makes it all. This hedgehog is an easy project to whip up for a last minute gift, and it's sure to bring a smile to any recipient!

what you'll need:

- G/6 (4.0 mm) crochet hook
- worsted weight yarn in light brown, dark brown, blue, and red
- fun fur in brown
- black safety eyes (9 mm)
- chenille needle

FINISHED SIZE: About 6 inches long

Instructions

BODY: Light brown yarn
• Make an adjustable ring.
Rnd 1: 4sc in ring (4)
Rnd 2: 1sc in each stitch (4)
Rnd 3: 2sc in each stitch (8)
Rnd 4: 1sc in each stitch (8)
Rnd 5: *2sc in next st, 1sc* (12) **(fig. 17a)**

Rnd 6: 1sc in each stitch (12)
Rnd 7: *2sc in next st, 2sc* (16)
Rnd 8: 1sc in each stitch (16)

Rnd 9: *2sc in next st, 3sc* (20)

Rnd 10–12: 1sc in each stitch (20)

Rnd 13: (2sc in next stitch) 10x, (1sc) 10x (30) **(fig. 17b)**

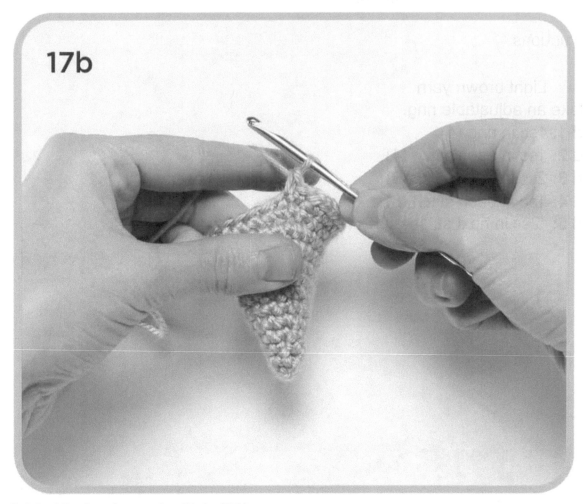

Rnd 14–16: 1sc in each stitch (30)

• Attach safety eyes on round 13.

Rnd 17–25: 1sc in each stitch (30)

• Begin stuffing. Stuff lightly in the nose, curling it up, and more firmly in the body. **(fig. 17c)**

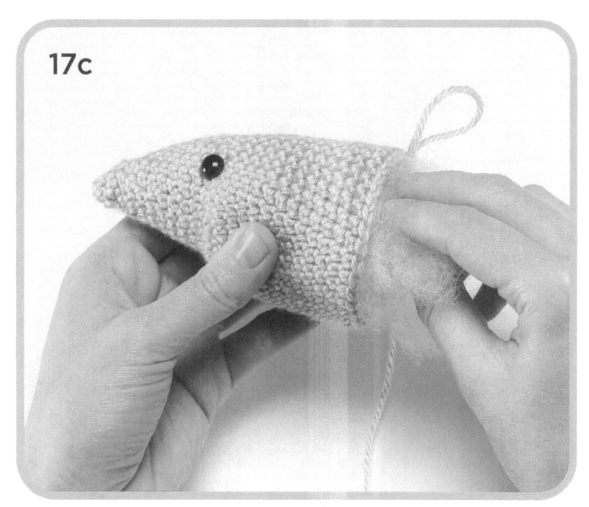

Rnd 26: *sc2tog, 3sc* (24)
Rnd 27: *sc2tog, 2sc* (18)
Rnd 28: *sc2tog, 1sc* (12)
• Finish stuffing.
Rnd 29: sc2tog in each stitch (6)
• Close with sl st and sew shut.

SPIKES: Brown fun fur

• Make an adjustable ring.

Rnd 1: 6sc in ring (6)

Rnd 2: 2sc in each stitch (12)

Rnd 3: *2sc in next st, 1sc* (18)

Rnd 4: *2sc in next st, 2sc* (24)

Rnd 5: *2sc in next st, 3sc* (30)

Rnd 6–11: 1sc in each stitch (30)

• Close with sl st, **(fig. 17d)** leaving a 6" tail for sewing. Optionally, turn the spikes inside out to make them even spikier!

FLOWER: Blue yarn
• Make an adjustable ring.
Rnd 1: 5sc in ring (5)
Rnd 2: *sl st, 2dc, sl st* (5)
• Close with sl st into first stitch.

FINISHING:
1. Arrange the spike on the top of the body and hold in place with pins.
2. Sew spikes all along the body, and weave in the ends. **(fig. 17e and 17f)**
3. With dark brown yarn, embroider the nose on the tip of the body.
4. Sew the flower onto the spikes with red yarn as shown in photo.

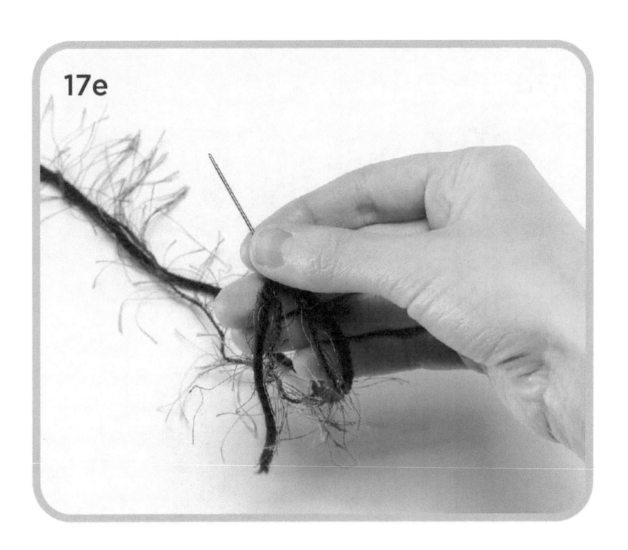

17e

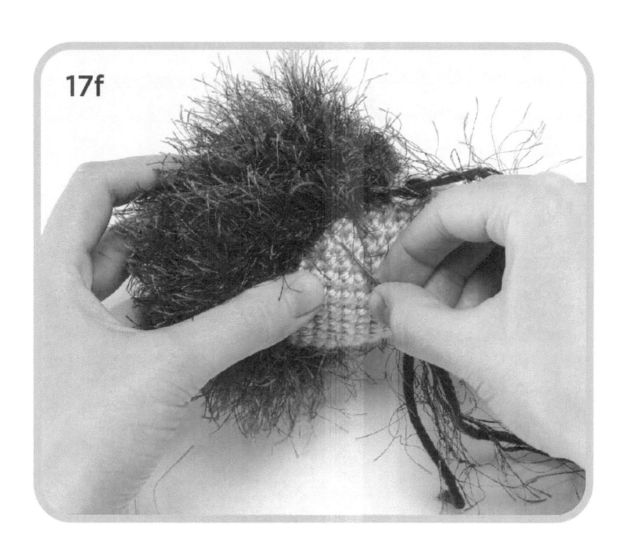

17f

cats

FROM PAULINE ABAYON IN ANTIPOLO CITY, PHILIPPINES

Each of Pauline's mischievous cats is fun on its own, but they tell a complete story as a group. By using a smaller hook size, it's possible to craft a cat that fits neatly in one of the trash cans—a perfect place to go digging for fish bones!

what you'll need:

- G/6 (4.0 mm), D/3 (3.25 mm), and B/1 (2.25 mm) crochet hooks
- worsted weight acrylic yarn in white, blue, black, pink, yellow, brown, and gray
- one pair wiggle eyes (12 mm) for black cat
- one pair wiggle eyes (10 mm) for each bone
- one black and one pink bead (4 mm)
- embroidery floss in black, blue, and brown
- chenille needle
- small needle for floss and beads
- stuffing
- craft glue and cardboard

FINISHED SIZE: Cats: 5 inches tall. Trash can: 4 inches tall. Fish bone: 3 inches long.

Instructions

CATS: Use a D/3 crochet hook for full-size cats; use a B/1 hook to make a smaller cat to fit inside a can.

HEAD (MAKE 3): Make one each in black, white, and yellow yarn.
• Make an adjustable ring.
Rnd 1: 6sc in ring (6)
Rnd 2: 2sc in each sc (12)
Rnd 3: *1sc, 2sc in next stitch* (18)
Rnd 4: *(1sc) 2x, 2sc in next stitch* (24)
Rnd 5: 1sc in each stitch (24)
Rnd 6: *(1sc) 3x, 2sc in next stitch* (30)
Rnd 7: 1sc in each stitch (30)
Rnd 8: *(1sc) 4x, 2sc in next stitch* (36)
Rnd 9–11: 1sc in each stitch (36)
Rnd 12: *(1sc) 4x, sc2tog* (30)
Rnd 13: 1sc in each stitch (30)
Rnd 14: *(1sc) 3x, sc2tog* (24)
Rnd 15: *(1sc) 2x, sc2tog* (18)
• Begin stuffing.
Rnd 16: *1sc, sc2tog* (12)

Rnd 17: sc2tog in each stitch (6)
• Close with sl st and finish stuffing, leaving a tail for sewing.

EARS (MAKE 6): Make two each in black (with pink), white (with blue), and yellow (with brown) yarn. When changing to inner ear color, hold the main color yarn behind the inner ear color.
• Make an adjustable ring.
Rnd 1: 6sc in ring (6)
Rnd 2: *1sc, 2sc in next stitch* (9)
Rnd 3: (1sc) 2x, 2sc in next stitch, 1sc
• Change to inner ear color: 2sc in next stitch. Change back to main color: 1sc, 2sc in next stitch, (1sc) 2x (12) **(fig. 18a)**

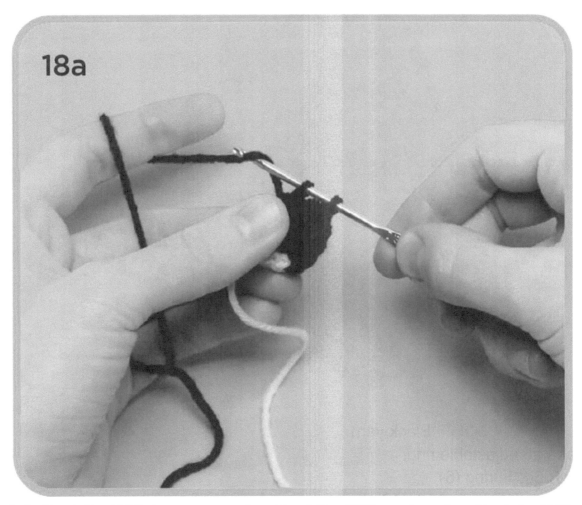

Rnd 4: (1sc) 5x. With inner ear color, (1sc) 3x. With main color, (1sc) 4x (12)
• Close with sl st in next sc, leaving a tail for sewing. Do not stuff ears.

SITTING CAT BODY: Black yarn

• Make an adjustable ring.

Rnd 1: 6sc in ring (6)

Rnd 2: 2sc in each stitch (12)

Rnd 3: *1sc, 2sc in next stitch* (18)

Rnd 4: *(1sc) 2x, 2sc in next stitch* (24)

Rnd 5: *(1sc) 5x, 2sc in next stitch* (28)

Rnd 6–9: 1sc in each stitch (28)

Rnd 10: *(1sc) 8x, (1sc, sc2tog) 4x, (1sc) 8x* (24) **(fig. 18b)**

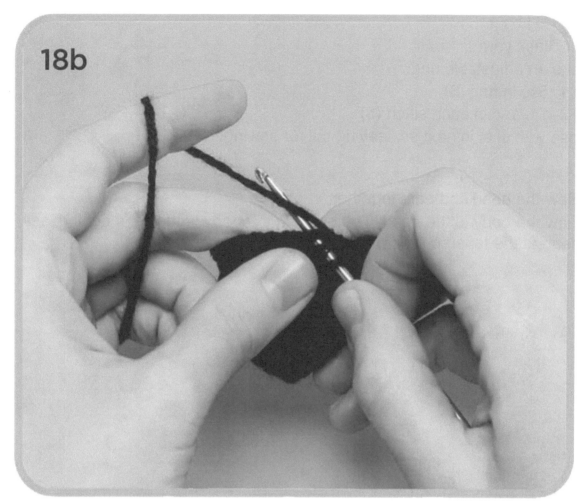

Rnd 11: *(1sc) 8x, (sc2tog) 4x, (1sc) 8x* (20)
Rnd 12: 1sc in each stitch (20)
Rnd 13: *(1sc) 8x, sc2tog* (18)
Rnd 14: *(1sc) 7x, sc2tog* (16)
Rnd 15: *(1sc) 6x, sc2tog* (14)
Rnd 16: *(1sc) 5x, sc2tog* (12)
Rnd 17: 1sc in each stitch (12)
• Close with sl st in next sc, leaving tail for sewing, and stuff.

FRONT LEGS (MAKE 2): Black yarn
• Make an adjustable ring.
Rnd 1: 6sc in ring (6)
Rnd 2–9: 1sc around, stuffing as you go (6).
• Close with sl st in next sc, leaving tail for sewing.

HIND LEGS (MAKE 2): Black yarn

- Follow the pattern for Front Legs up to Rnd 6. Close with sl st in next sc, leaving tail for sewing.

TAIL: Black yarn
- Make an adjustable ring.
Rnd 1: 5sc in ring (5)
Rnd 2–14: 1sc in each stitch (5)
- Close with sl st in next sc, leaving tail for sewing.

FINISHING:
1. Sew the head and ears together.
2. Sew the body to the head. The bulge in the body is the cat's behind; sew head at the tapered (neck) end. **(fig. 18c)**

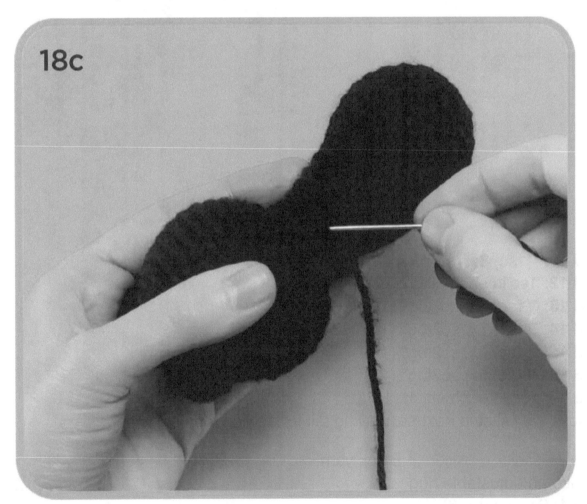

3. Sew the hind legs near the base of the body, towards the front. Sew the front legs in place, in front of the body.
4. Sew the tail at the back.
5. Glue the eyes on the face with craft glue.

6. Stitch on a pink bead for the nose using black floss. Stitch three short whiskers on each side of the face using brown floss.

PLAYFUL CAT BODY: White yarn

Rnd 1–14: Sitting Cat body.

Rnd 15–20: 1sc around (16).

• Close with sl st in next sc, leaving the tail for sewing, and stuff.

FRONT LEGS, HIND LEGS, AND TAIL:

• Follow the same patterns as for Sitting Cat, using white yarn.

FINISHING:

1. Sew the head and ears together.
2. Flatten the end of the body and sew it closed. Sew it to the head.
3. Sew the hind legs near the base of the body, at the back. Sew the front legs near the base of the body towards the front.
4. Sew tail at the back.
5. Embroider eyes with blue floss. Stitch a short curved line for her smile. Stitch three short whiskers on each side of the face.

CAT INSIDE THE CAN BODY: Yellow yarn

Rnd 1–4: Sitting Cat body
Rnd 5: 1sc in each stitch (24)
Rnd 6: *(1sc) 4x, sc2tog* (20)
Rnd 7: *(1sc) 3x, sc2tog* (16)
Rnds 8–11: 1sc in each stitch (16)
• Close with sl st in next sc and stuff, leaving the tail for sewing.

LEGS (MAKE 4): Yellow yarn
• Make adjustable ring.
Rnd 1: 6sc in ring (6)
Rnd 2–6: 1sc around, stuffing as you go (6)
• Close with sl st in next sc and stuff, leaving the tail for sewing.

FINISHING:
1. Sew the head and ears together.
2. Sew the body to the head.
3. Stitch stripes on top of the head and on the sides of the body using brown yarn. **(fig. 18d)**

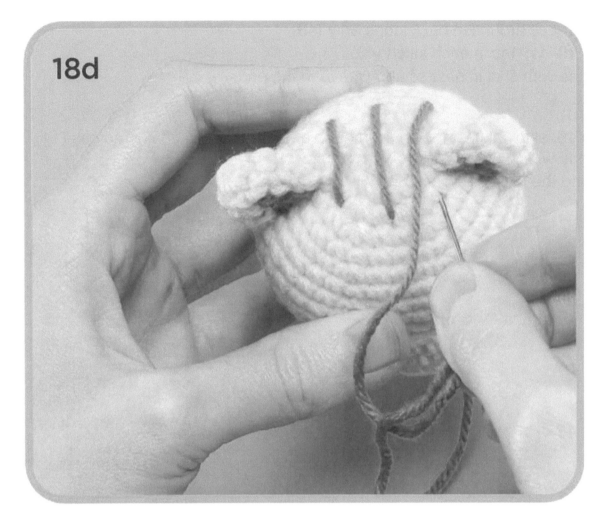

4. Sew the legs in place.

5. Embroider the eyes with blue floss.

6. Sew short whiskers on each side of the face. Sew on a black bead for the nose.

TRASH CAN: G/6 crochet hook, gray yarn

COVER:

• Make an adjustable ring.

Rnd 1: 6sc in ring (6)

Rnd 2: 2sc in each stitch (12)

Rnd 3: *1sc, 2sc in next stitch* (18)

Rnd 4: *2sc in next stitch, (1sc) 2x* (24)

Rnd 5: *(1sc) 3x, 2sc in next stitch* (30)

Rnd 6: (1sc) 2x, (2sc in next stitch, 4sc) 5x, 2sc in next stitch, (1sc) 2x (36)

Rnd 7: *2sc in next st, (1sc) 5x* (42)

Rnd 8: (1sc) 3x, (2sc in next stitch, 6sc) 5x, 2sc in next stitch, (1sc) 3x (48)

Rnd 9: 1sc around in back loops only (48)

Rnd 10–11: 1sc in each stitch (48)

• Close with sl st in next sc and weave in the ends.

HANDLE:

• Ch 15, skip 1st chain, then sc in each of the remaining chains across (14).
  Close with sl st,

leaving the tail for sewing.

CAN:

Rnd 1–8: As for cover.

Rnd 9: 1dc in back loops only (48)
Rnd 10: *1fpdc, bpdc* (48) **(fig. 18e and 18f)**

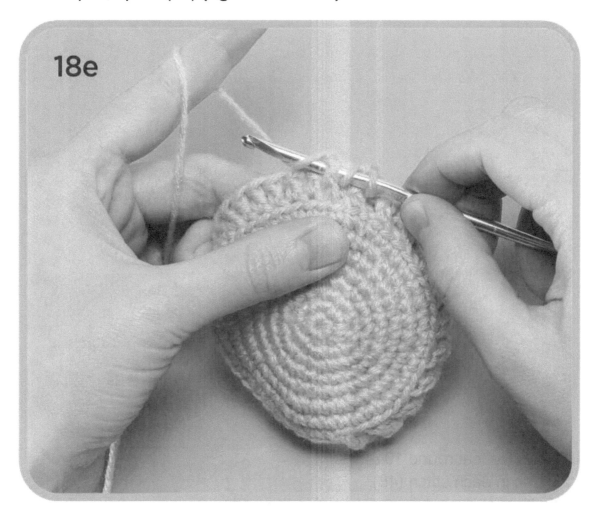

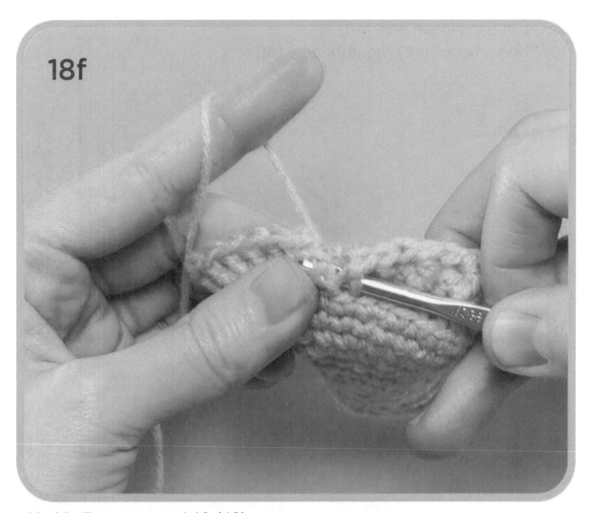

Rnd 11–22: Repeat round 10 (48)

Rnd 23: 1sc in each stitch (48).

• Close with sl st in next sc and weave in the ends.

FINISHING:

1. Sew both ends of the handle to the cover.
2. Cut a piece of cardboard (3" x 7") and put inside the trash can to serve as support.

FISH: D/3 crochet hook, any color yarn

HEAD:
• Make an adjustable ring.
Rnd 1: 6sc in ring (6)
Rnd 2: *1sc, 2sc in next stitch* (9)
Rnd 3: *1sc 2x, 2sc in next stitch* (12)
Rnd 4: *1sc 3x, 2sc in next stitch* (15) **(fig. 18g)**

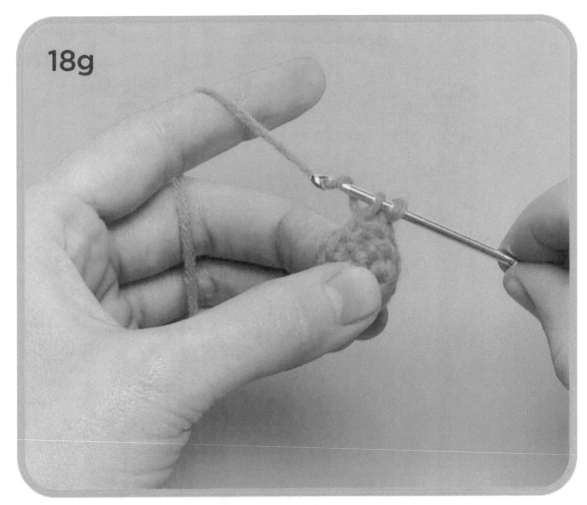

Rnd 5: *1sc 4x, 2sc in next stitch* (18)
Rnd 6: *1sc 5x, 2sc in next stitch* (21)
• Close with sl st in next sc, leaving the tail for sewing.

TAIL:
Rnds 1–3: Follow Fish Head
• Close with sl st in next sc, leaving the tail for sewing.

BACKBONE:
• Make an adjustable ring.
Rnd 1: 4sc in ring (4)
Rnds 2–10: 1sc in each stitch (4)
• Close with sl st in next sc, leaving the tail for sewing.

SIDE BONES (MAKE 4):
• Follow the Backbone pattern up to Rnd 3 only. Finish off, leaving tail for sewing.

FINISHING:

1. Insert part of the backbone into the fish head and sew together.

2. Sew the other end of the backbone to the fish tail.

3. Sew the short bones to the sides of the backbone.

4. Glue on eyes with craft glue.

fox

FROM KANDICE SORAYA GROTE IN CALIFORNIA

Are you feeling foxy? Courtesy of Kandice Soraya Grote, this little fox is ready to give you a big hug and join your group of furry friends.

what you'll need:

- F/5 (3.75 mm) crochet hook
- worsted weight yarn in orange, black, and white
- chenille needle
- black safety eyes (6 mm)

FINISHED SIZE: About 3$^1/_2$ inches tall

Instructions

HEAD: Start with orange yarn
• Make an adjustable ring.
Rnd 1: 7sc in ring (7)
Rnd 2: 2sc in each st (14)
Rnd 3: *1sc, 2sc in next st* (21)
Rnd 4–6: 1sc in each st (21)
• Change to White yarn.
Rnd 7: 1sc in each st (21)
Rnd 8: *5sc, sc2tog* (18)
Rnd 9: *4sc, sc2tog* (15)
• Attach safety eyes between rounds 5 and 6.
Rnd 10: *3sc, sc2tog* (12)
• Stuff firmly.
Rnd 11: *2sc, sc2tog* (9) **(fig. 19a)**

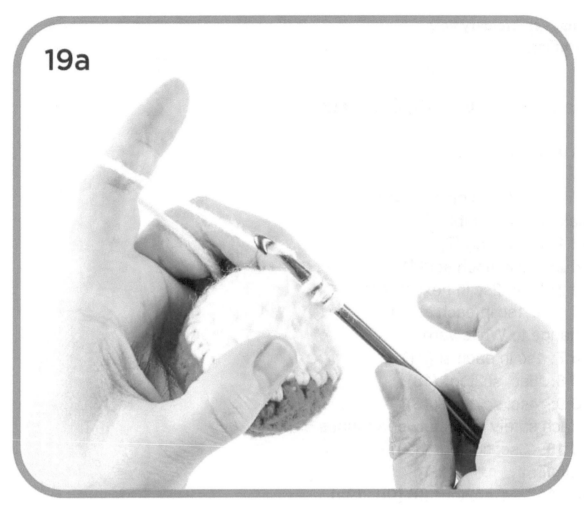

19a

Rnd 12: *skip 1 st, sc2tog* (6)
• Stuff head and finish off.

NOSE: Orange yarn
• Make an adjustable ring.
Rnd 1: 5sc in ring (5)
Rnd 2: sc in each st (5)
• Finish off, leaving a long tail for sewing into head.
• Use black embroidery thread to sew on a nose and smile. **(fig. 19b)**

19b

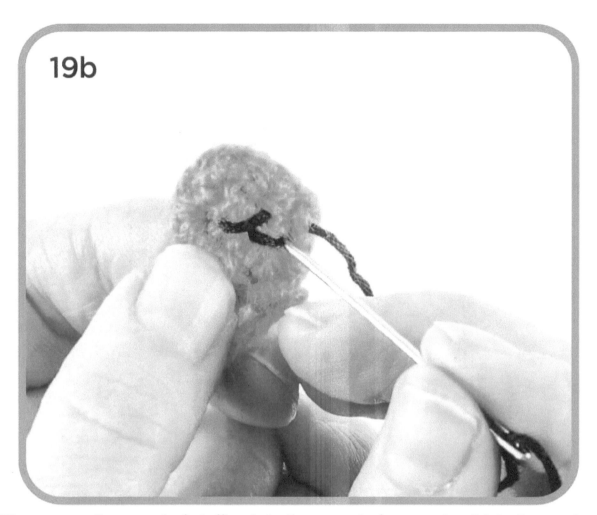

• Place a small amount of stuffing into the nose before sewing it into the center of the head.

EARS (MAKE 2): Start with black yarn

• Make an adjustable ring.

Rnd 1: 1sc (5x) in ring (5)

Rnd 2: sc in each st (5)

• Change to Orange yarn.

Rnd 3: *1sc, 2sc in next st* (2x), sc (7)

Rnd 4–6: 1sc in each st (7)

Rnd 7: 1sc, sc2tog (3x) (3)

• Finish off, leaving a long tail for sewing. Do not stuff.

BODY: Orange yarn
• Make an adjustable ring.
Rnd 1: 7sc in ring (7)
Rnd 2: 2sc in each st (14)
Rnd 3: *1sc, 2sc in the next st* (21)
Rnd 4–5: 1sc in each st (21)
Rnd 6: (3sc, sc2tog) 4x, 1sc (17) **(fig. 19c)**

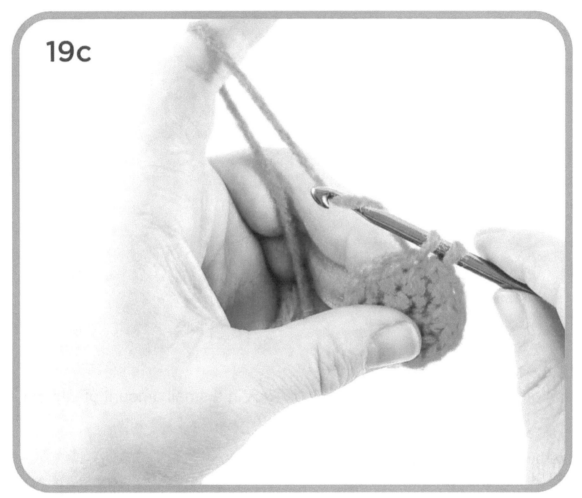

19c

Rnd 7: (2sc, sc2tog) 4x, 1sc (13)
Rnd 8: (1sc, sc2tog) 3x, 1sc (9)
Rnd 9: (1sc, sc2tog) 2x, sc (6)
• Stuff body firmly and finish off.

ARMS (MAKE 2): Start with black yarn
• Make an adjustable ring.
Rnd 1: 5sc in ring (5)
Rnd 2–4: 1sc in each st (5)

• Change to orange yarn. **(fig. 19d)**

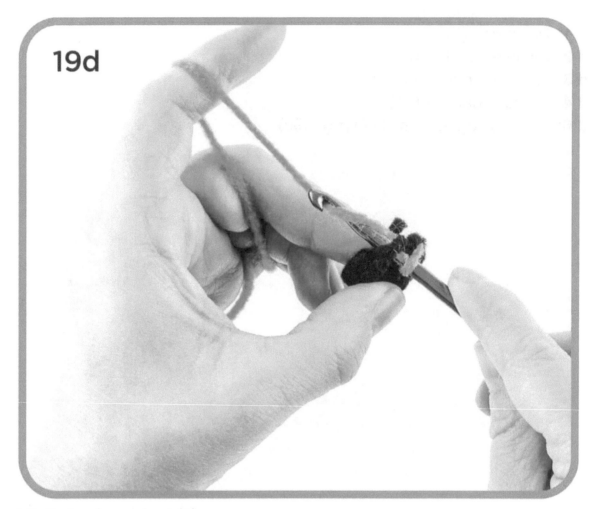

Rnd 5–6: 1sc in each st (5)
• Finish off, leaving a long tail for sewing. Tuck in a small amount of stuffing.

FEET (MAKE 2): Black yarn
• Make an adjustable ring.
Rnd 1: 5sc in ring (5)
Rnd 2–4: 1sc in each st (5)
• Finish off, leaving a long tail for sewing. Tuck in a small amount of stuffing.

TAIL: Start white yarn
• Make an adjustable ring.
Rnd 1: 6sc in ring (6)
Rnd 2: 1sc in each st (6)
Rnd 3: *1sc, 2sc in the next st (9)
Rnd 4: *2sc, 2sc in the next st* (12)
Rnd 5: sc in each st (12)

- Change to orange yarn.
Rnd 6: 1sc in each st. (12)
Rnd 7: *4sc, sc2tog* (10)
- Stuff firmly. **(fig. 19e)**

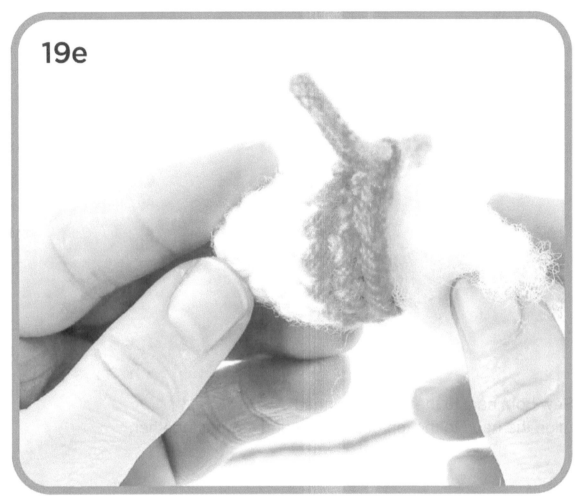

Rnd 8: *3sc, sc2tog* (8)
Rnd 9–10: 1sc in each st (8)
Rnd 11: *2sc, sc2tog* (6)
Rnd 12: 1sc in each st (6)
Rnd 13: 1sc, sc2tog, 2sc (5)
- Finish off, leaving a long tail. Complete stuffing.

FINISHING:
1. Sew the legs and tail into the body. **(fig. 19f)**

19f

2. Sew both ears to the top of the head

3. Align the head to the top of the body and sewing together.

raccoon

FROM KANDICE SORAYA GROTE IN CALIFORNIA

This adorable raccoon is another one of Kandice's cute creations. But watch out, friends, because this little bandit will steal your heart away!

what you'll need:

- **F/5 (3.75 mm) crochet hook**
- **worsted weight acrylic yarn in black and gray**
- **black embroidery thread**
- **felt in black and gray**

- **black safety eyes (6 mm)**
- **chenille needle**
- **craft glue**
- **stuffing**

FINISHED SIZE: About 3$^1/_2$ inches tall

Instructions

For the mask, cut two white ovals and two black ovals from felt using the template shown here. Make a small hole in each set of ovals for the safety eyes. Add a little glue between layers tothem aligned.

HEAD: Gray yarn
- Make an adjustable ring.

Rnd 1: 7sc in ring (7)

Rnd 2: 2sc in each st (14)

Rnd 3: *1sc, 2sc in next st* (21)

Rnd 4–7: 1sc in each st (21)

Rnd 8: *5sc, sc2tog* (18)

Rnd 9: *4sc, sc2tog* (15)

- Attach the felt mask and safety eyes between rounds 6 and 7. Secure the safety eyes through both layers of felt and the crocheted work. **(fig. 20a)**

20a

Rnd 10: *3sc, sc2tog* (12)
• Stuff firmly.
Rnd 11: *2sc, sc2tog* (9)
Rnd 12: *1sc, sc2tog* (6)
• Stuff and finish off.

NOSE: Gray yarn
• Make an adjustable ring.
Rnd 1: 5sc in ring (5)
Rnd 2: 1sc in each st (5)
• Finish off, leaving a long tail for sewing.
• Use Black embroidery thread to sew in a nose and smile. **(fig. 20b)**

20b

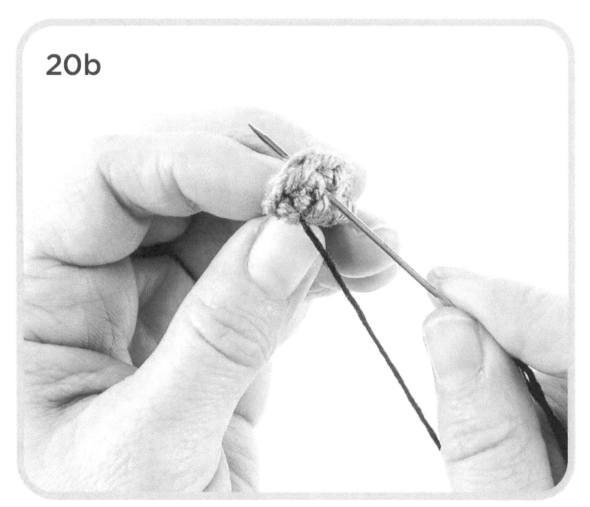

- Place a small amount of stuffing into the nose before placing it in the center of the head and sewing it into place.

EARS (MAKE 2): Start with black yarn
- Make an adjustable ring.
Rnd 1: 6sc in ring (6)
Rnd 2: 1sc in each st (6)
- Change to gray yarn. **(fig. 20c)**

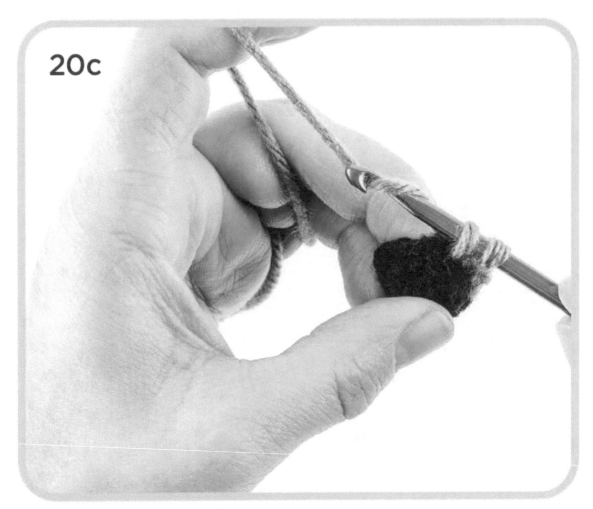

Rnd 3: *1sc, 2sc in next st* (9)

Rnd 4: 1sc in each st (9)

• Leaving unstuffed, finish off, leaving a long tail for sewing.

BODY: Gray yarn

• Make an adjustable ring.

Rnd 1: 7sc in ring (7)

Rnd 2: 2sc in each st (14)

Rnd 3: *1sc, 2sc in the next st* (21)

Rnd 4–5: 1sc in each st (21)

Rnd 6: (3sc, sc2tog) 4x, 1sc (17) **(fig. 20d)**

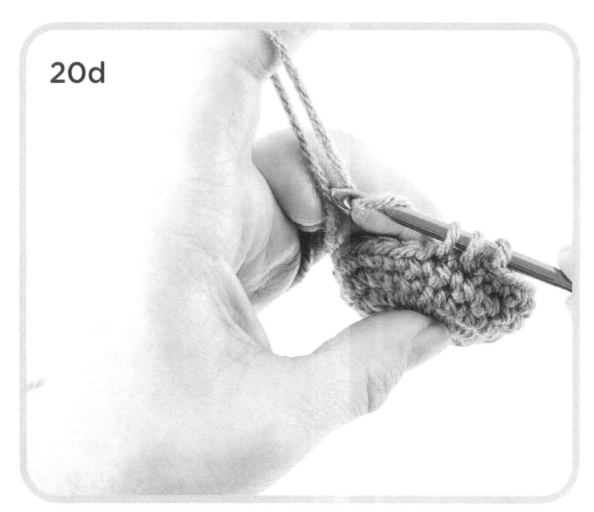

20d

Rnd 7: (2sc, sc2tog) 3x, 1sc (13)
Rnd 8: (1sc, sc2tog) 4x, 1sc (9)
Rnd 9: (1sc, sc2tog) 2x, 1sc (6)
• Stuff body firmly and finish off.

ARMS (MAKE 2): Start with black yarn
• Make an adjustable ring.
Rnd 1: 5sc in ring (5)
Rnd 2–4: 1sc in each st (5)
• Change to gray yarn.
Rnds 5-6: 1sc in each st (5) **(fig. 20e)**

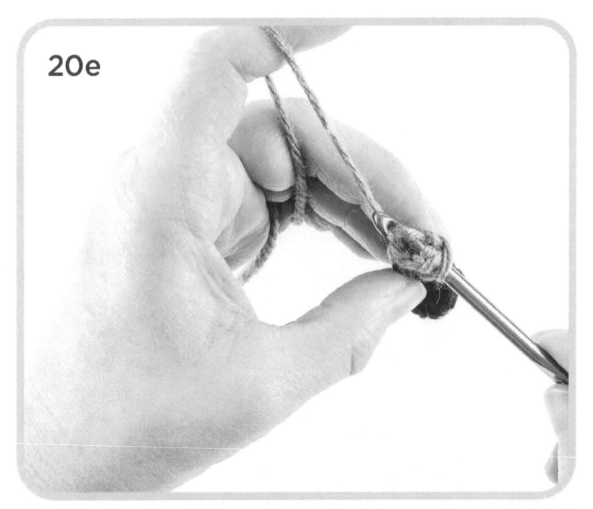

20e

• Finish off, leaving a long tail for sewing, and tuck in a small amount of stuffing.

FEET (MAKE 2): Black yarn
• Make an adjustable ring.
Rnd 1: 5sc in ring (5)
Rnd 2–4: 1sc in each st (5)
• Finish off, leaving a long tail for sewing, and tuck in a small amount of stuffing.

TAIL: Start with gray yarn
• Make an adjustable ring.
Rnd 1: 6sc in ring (6)
Rnd 2: 1sc in each st (6)
Rnd 3: *1sc, 2sc in the next st* (9)
• Change to black yarn.
Rnd 4: *2sc, 2sc in the next st* (12)
Rnd 5: 1sc in each st (12)
• Change to gray yarn.

Rnd 6: 1sc in each st (12)
• Change to black yarn.
Rnd 7: *4sc, sc2tog* (10)
• Change to gray yarn.
• Stuff firmly.
Rnd 8: *3sc, sc2tog* (8)
• Change to black yarn. **(fig. 20f)**

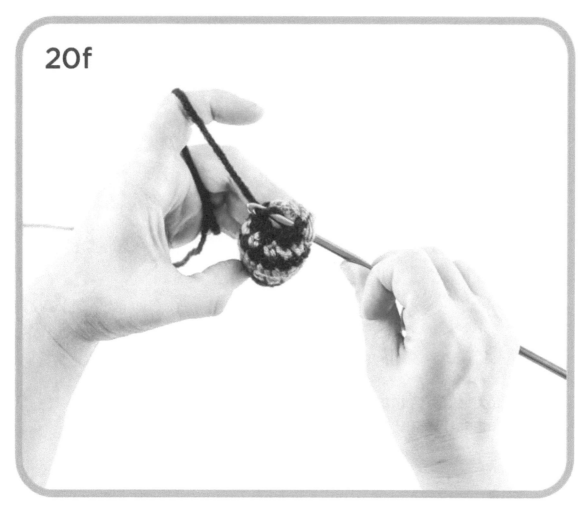

20f

Rnd 9: 1sc in each st (8)
• Change to gray yarn.
Rnd 10: 1sc in each st (8)
• Change to black yarn.
Rnd 11: *2sc, sc2tog* (6)
Rnd 12: 1sc in each st (6)
Rnd 13: 1sc, sc2tog, 2sc (5)
• Finish off and stuff, leaving a long tail for sewing.

FINISHING:

1. Sew the arms, legs, and tail to the body. **(fig. 20g)**

2. Sew ears to the top of the head.

3. Aligning the head to the top of the body and sewing together.

fawn

FROM RACHELLE SMITH IN SALT LAKE CITY, UTAH

Foraging for your own food can be a lot of work when you're young, so sometimes you just gotta take a nap! Make a diorama with it, give it to your kid to snuggle with at night, or give it to a fawn lover in your life (we all have one!).

what you'll need:

- F/5 (3.75mm) crochet hook
- worsted weight acrylic yarn in tan, black and white
- black safety eyes (12 mm)
- chenille needle
- stuffing

FINISHED SIZE: About 6 inches long

Instructions

HEAD: Start with black yarn
• Make an adjustable ring.
Rnd 1: 3sc into ring
• Change to tan yarn (3)
Rnd 2–3: 1sc in each st (3)
Rnd 4: 2sc in each st (6)
Rnd 5: 2sc in each st (12)
Rnd 6: *1sc, 2sc in next st* (18)
Rnd 7: *2sc, 2sc in next st* (24) **(fig. 21a)**

Rnd 8: 1sc in each st (24)
Rnd 9: *2sc, sc2tog* (18)
Rnd 10: *1sc, sc2tog* (12)

• Attach safety eyes between rounds 10 and 11. Stuff firmly.

Rnd 11: *sc2tog* (6)

Rnd 12: *sc2tog* (3)

• Finish off, leaving a tail, and sew the head closed.

BODY: Tan yarn

• Make an adjustable ring.

Rnd 1: 5sc in ring (5)

Rnd 2: 2sc in each st (10)

Rnd 3: 1sc in each st (10)

Rnd 4: *1sc, 2sc in next st* (15)

Rnd 5: *2sc, 2sc in next st* (20)

Rnd 6: 1sc in each st (20)

Rnd 7: *3sc, 2sc in next st* (25)

Rnd 8–11: 1sc in each st

Rnd 12: *3sc, sc2tog* (20)

Rnd 13: 1sc in each st (20)

Rnd 14: *2sc, sc2tog* (15)

Rnd 15: 1sc in each st (15)

• Stuff firmly.

Rnd 16: *sc, sc2tog* (10)

Rnd 17: *sc2tog* (5)

Rnd 18–19: 1sc in each st (5)

• Finish off, leaving a tail for sewing.

• Stuff neck, and sew the head to the body.

EAR (MAKE 2): Tan yarn

Note: This piece is completed in one row worked around the foundation chain.

• ch 6, start in 2nd ch from hook.

Row 1: 2sc, dc, sc, 2sc in next st, then continuing around the chain, sc, dc, 2sc (10) **(fig. 21b)**

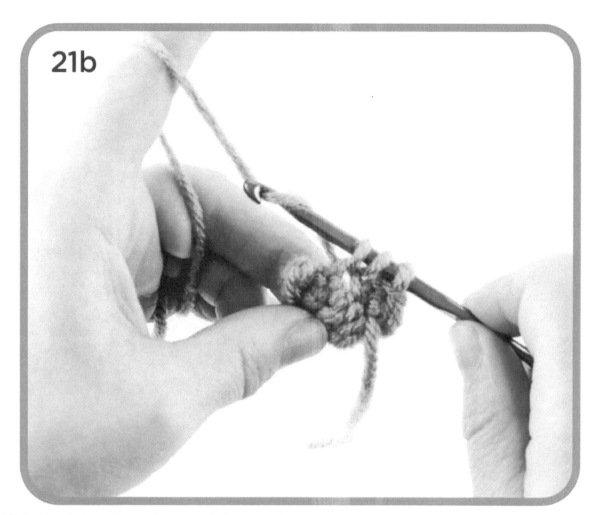

21b

• Finish off, leaving a long tail for sewing.

INNER EAR (MAKE 2): White yarn

• Ch 6, start in 2nd ch from hook.

Row 1: 2sc, dc, sc, sl st (4)

• Finish off, leaving a tail to sew onto the outer ears.

• Sew into the outer ear **(fig. 21c)** and then sew the ear to the head.

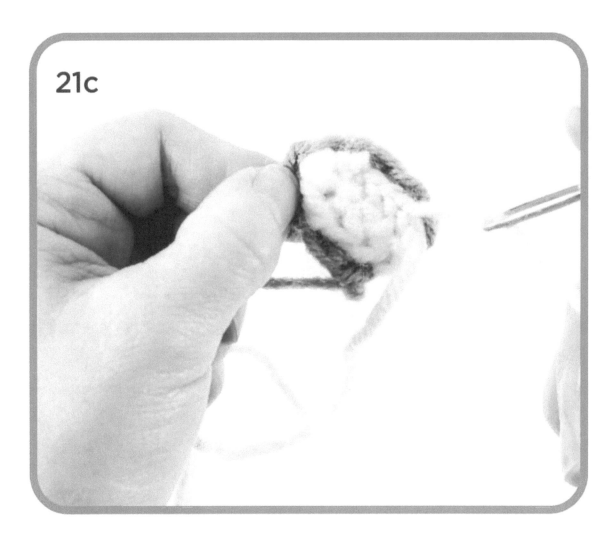

21c

LEGS (MAKE 4): Start with black yarn
• Make an adjustable ring.
Rnd 1: 4sc into ring (4)
Rnd 2: 1sc in each st
• Change to tan yarn. (4)
Rnd 3–12: 1sc in each st (4)
• Finish off, leaving a long tail.

HAUNCH (MAKE 2): Tan yarn
• Ch 4. Working in rows, start in 2nd ch from hook.
Row 1: 1sc across, ch 1, turn (3)
Row 2: 2sc in next st, sc, 2sc in next st ch 1, turn (5)
Row 3: 1sc, 2sc in next st, sc, 2sc in next st, sc, ch 1, turn (7) **(fig. 21d)**

21d

Row 4: sc, 2sc in next st, 3sc, 2sc in next st, sc, ch1, turn (9)
Row 5: sc in each st (9)

• Finish off, leaving a long tail.
• Sew the haunch across the top of a leg **(fig. 21e)**, starting at the end of the leg to form a completed back leg. Repeat for second back leg.

21e

- Sew back legs to the back end of the body **(fig. 21f)**, stuffing the haunches before closing.

21f

- Line up the two remaining legs under the head and sew to the underside of the body.

TAIL (MAKE 2): One with tan yarn, one with white yarn
- Ch 6, start in 2nd ch from hook.

Row 1: 2sc, dc, sc, sl st (5)

- Finish it off, leaving a tail.
- Sew the two pieces together with the tan yarn tail, and then sew it to the body. **(fig. 21g)**

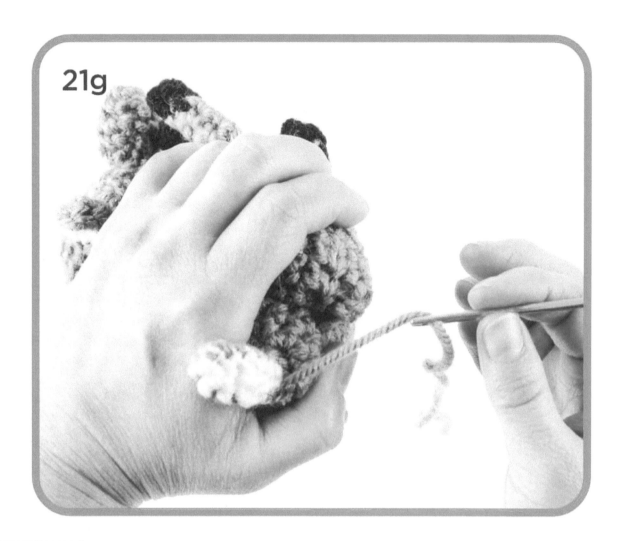

FINISHING:

1. With black yarn, sew two small "v" shapes on the outer edges of the eyes to create eyelashes.

2. With about 20 inches of white yarn, sew little dashes onto the fawn's back to create the spots. Keep them spread out mainly on the top of the back toward the tail **(fig. 21h)**. Now you've created a beautiful fawn!

21h

squirrel

FROM ALICIA KACHMAR IN PENNSYLVANIA

While they are adorable, squirrels have no qualms about running up your leg to steal your burrito. When I saw this adorable squirrel designed by Alicia, though, I thought, "Now this is a squirrel I can get behind." Adorable, friendly, AND it's already occupied with its own acorn, so I can eat my burrito in peace.

what you'll need:

- G/6 (4.25 mm) and K/10.5 (6.5 mm) crochet hooks
- worsted weight acrylic yarn in gray, olive green, black and tan

- bulky weight yarn in off-white
- wool roving in gray
- black safety eyes (8 mm)
- needle-felting needle
- chenille needle
- stuffing
- fabric glue (optional)

FINISHED SIZE: About $5^1/_2$ inches tall

Instructions

ACORN BASE: Green yarn
• Using G/6 hook, ch 2, start in 2nd ch from hook.
Rnd 1: 4sc (4)
Rnd 2: 2sc in each st (8)
Rnd 3: 2sc in first st, 7sc (9)
Rnd 4: 1sc in each st (9)
Rnd 5: *sc2tog, sc* and sl st to next st (6)
• Finish off and weave in the ends.

ACORN TOP: Tan yarn
• Using G/6 hook and leaving a long tail, ch 2, start in 2nd ch from hook.
Rnd 1: 4sc (4)
Rnd 2: 2sc in each st (8)
Rnd 3: (2sc in next st, 1sc) 4x, sl st to next st (12)
• Finish off, leaving a long tail.
• To make the stem, pull up the first long tail through the center, ch 3, 1sc in 2nd and 3rd ch from hook, sl st into round 1, finish off. **(fig. 22a)**

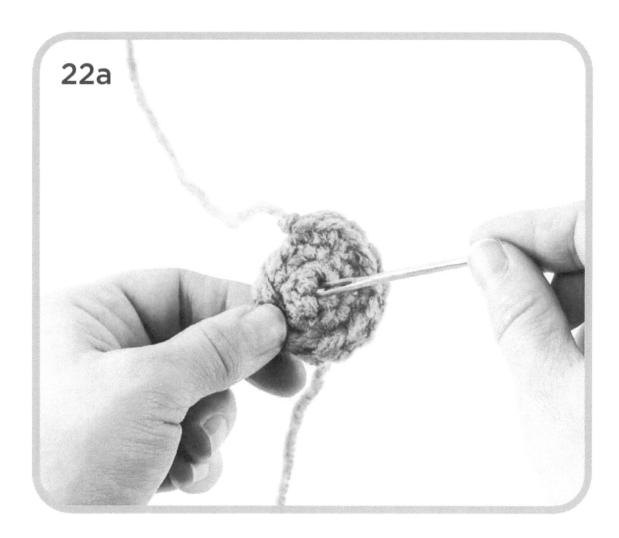

BODY: Gray yarn

• Using G/6 hook, ch 2, start in 2nd ch from hook.

Rnd 1: 5sc (5)

Rnd 2: 2sc in each st (10)

Rnd 3: *2sc in next st, 1sc* (15)

Rnd 4: 1sc in each st (15)

Rnd 5: *2sc in next st, 2sc* (20)

Rnd 6: 1sc in each st (20)

Rnd 7: *2sc in next st, 3sc* (25)

Rnd 8–10: 1sc in each st (25)

Rnd 11: *sc2tog, 3sc* (20)

Rnd 12: 1sc in each st (20)

Rnd 13: *sc2tog, 3sc* (16) **(fig. 22b)**

Rnd 14: 1sc in each st (16)

Rnd 15: *sc2tog, 2sc* (12)

• Stuff the body and finish off, leaving an 8-inch tail for sewing.

EARS (MAKE 2): Gray yarn

• Using G/6 hook, ch 3, start in 2nd ch from hook.

Rnd 1: ehdc in 2nd and 3rd ch from hook, ch 1 and sl to first ch (3) **(fig. 22c)**

22c

• Finish off, leaving a 4-inch tail for sewing.

NOSE: Black yarn
• Using G/6 hook, ch 2.
Rnd 1: sl in first ch (1)
• Finish off, leaving a 4-inch tail for sewing.

HEAD: Gray yarn
• Using G/6 hook, ch 2, start in 2nd ch from hook.
Rnd 1: 3sc (3)
Rnd 2: 2sc in each st (6)
Rnd 3: 1sc in each st (6)
Rnd 4: *2sc in next st, sc* (9)
Rnd 5: 1sc in each st (9)
Rnd 6: *2sc in next st, 2sc* (12)
Rnd 7: *2sc in next st, 3sc* (15)
Rnd 8: *2sc in next st, 4sc* (18)

Rnd 9: 1sc in each st (18) **(fig. 22d)**

22d

Rnd 10: *sc2tog, 4sc* (15)

Rnd 11: *sc2tog, sc* (10)

• Sew on nose and ears, and attach safety eyes between rounds 6 and 7. Stuff the head.

Rnd 12: *sc2tog* (5)

• Finish off, leaving a tail for sewing.

ARMS (MAKE 2): Gray yarn

• Using G/6 hook, ch 2, start in 2nd ch from hook.

Rnd 1: 3sc (3)

Rnd 2–8: 1sc in each st (3)

• Finish off, leaving a 4-inch tail for sewing.

FEET BOTTOMS (MAKE 2): Gray yarn

• Using G hook, ch 2, start in 2nd ch from hook.

Rnd 1: 1sc 5x (5)

Rnd 2: 2sc in first st, (1sc) 4x (6)
Rnd 3–4: 1sc in each st (6)
Rnd 5: sc2tog, (1sc) 4x (5) **(fig. 22e)**

• Finish off, leaving a 4-inch tail for sewing.

LEGS (MAKE 2): Gray yarn
• Using G/6 hook, ch 2, start in 2nd ch from hook.
Rnd 1: 6sc (6)
Rnd 2: 2sc in each st (12)
Rnd 3–6: 1sc in each st (12)
Rnd 7: *sc2tog, 2sc* (9)
• Stuff legs and finish off, leaving a 12-inch tail for sewing.

BELLY: Off-White yarn
• Using K/10.5 hook, ch 3, start in 2nd ch from hook. Work back and forth in rows, turning work.
Row 1: 1sc in 2nd and 3rd ch from hook, ch 1, turn (2)

Row 2: 1sc in each st, ch 1, turn (2)
Row 3: 2sc in first st, sc, ch 1, turn (3)
Row 4: 1sc in each st, ch 1, turn (3)
Row 5: sc2tog, sc, ch 1, turn (2) **(fig. 22f)**

22f

Row 6–7: 1sc in each st, ch 1, turn (2)
Row 8: sc2tog, ch 1 (1)

• Working around the outside of the belly, 1sc in each st. Work 2sc into row 1 and sl st to fasten off. **(fig. 22g)**

22g

• Leave a 10-inch tail for sewing.

FINISHING:
1. Stuff the acorn and sew on the top.
2. Sew the belly piece to the body
3. Sew the feet to the legs, allowing half of each foot to stick out from the leg.
4. Sew legs and arms to the sides of the body, and sew the head to the body.
5. Stretch out a 6-inch by 3-inch piece of gray wool roving. Using felting needle, tack roving to the backside of the body. **(fig. 22h)**

22h

6. With extra yarn or glue, attach the acorn to the ends of arms.

kitten

FROM DENISE FERGUSON OF YUMMY PANCAKE IN PENNSYLVANIA

This itty-bitty kitty makes a great house pet—she's well groomed and completely potty trained, and she won't claw your furniture. Basically, she's the purrfect kitten. Designed by Denise Ferguson, this little kitty is the cat's meow!

what you'll need:

- G/6 (4.0 mm) crochet hook

- **worsted weight acrylic yarn in gray, pink, and black**
- **cat safety eyes (15 mm)**
- **fishing line**
- **chenille needle**
- **stuffing**

FINISHED SIZE: About 6$^1/_2$ inches tall

Instructions

EARS (MAKE 2): Gray yarn
- Make an adjustable ring.
Rnd 1: 6sc in ring (6)
Rnd 2: 2sc in each stitch (12)
Rnd 3: *1sc, 2sc in next st* (18)
Rnds 4–6: 1sc in each st (18)
- Sl st and finish off, leaving a long tail for sewing.

ARMS (MAKE 2): Gray yarn
- Make an adjustable ring.
Rnd 1: 6sc in ring (6)
Rnd 2: *1sc, 2sc in next st* (9)
Rnds 3–9: 1sc in each st (9)
- Finish off, leaving a long tail for sewing.

LEGS (MAKE 2): Gray yarn
- Make an adjustable ring.
Rnd 1: 6sc in ring (6)
Rnd 2: 2sc in each stitch (12)
Rnds 3–4: 1sc in each st (12)
Rnds 5–6: (1sc) 4x, (1 sl st) 4x, (1sc) 4x (12)
Rnd 7: (1sc) 4x, (1 sl st) 4x, (1sc) 2x, (1hdc) 2x (12) **(fig. 23a)**

Rnd 8: (1hdc) 2x, (1sc) 10x (12)
Rnds 9–11: 1sc in each st (12)
Rnd 10: (sc2tog) 6x (6)
• Finish off, leaving a long tail for sewing.

TAIL: Gray yarn
• Make an adjustable ring.
Rnd 1: 6sc in ring (6)
Rnds 2–27: 1sc in each st (6)
• Finish off, leaving a long tail for sewing.

SNOUT: Gray yarn
Rnd 1: ch 4, 1sc in 2nd ch from hook, 1sc in next st, 3sc in next st, 1sc in next st, 2sc in next st (8) **(fig. 23b)**

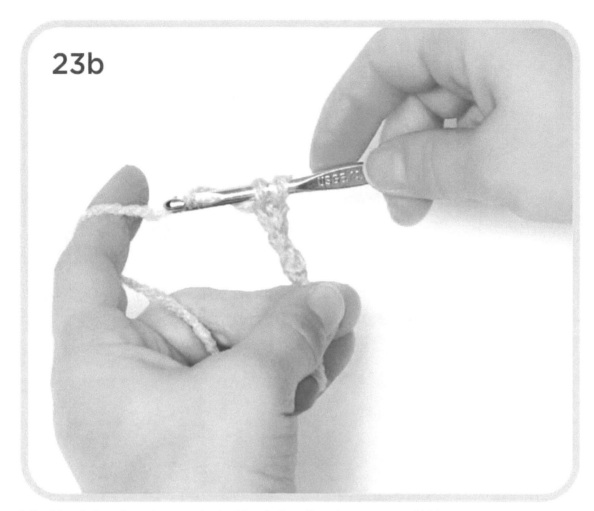

23b

Rnd 2: (1sc) 3x, 2sc in next st, (1sc) 3x, 2sc in next st (10)

Rnd 3: (1sc) 4x, 2sc in next st, (1sc) 4x, 2sc in next st (12)

- Finish off, leaving a long tail for sewing.
- Using pink yarn, sew on the nose, and using black yarn, sew on the mouth. **(fig. 23c)**

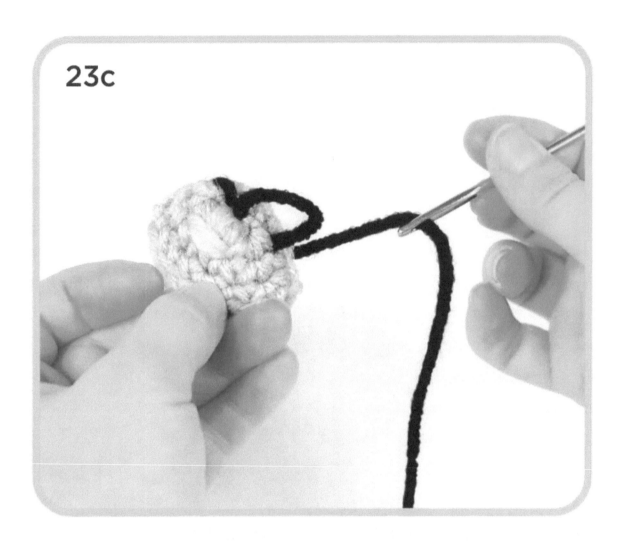

23c

HEAD: Gray yarn

• Make an adjustable ring.

Rnd 1: 6sc in ring (6)

Rnd 2: 2sc in each stitch (12)

Rnd 3: *1sc, 2sc in next st* (18)

Rnd 4: *(1sc) 2x, 2sc in next st* (24)

Rnd 5: *(1sc) 3x, 2sc in next st* (30)

Rnd 6: *(1sc) 4x, 2sc in next st* (36)

Rnds 7–11: 1 sc in each st (36)

• Sew on the ears, add the safety eyes, and sew on the snout. **(fig. 23d)**

23d

- Cut fishing line and thread it into the snout to make whiskers.
- Stuff the head firmly.

Rnd 12: *(1sc) 4x, sc2tog* (30)
Rnd 13: *(1sc) 3x, sc2tog* (24)
Rnd 14: *(1sc) 2x, sc2tog* (18)
Rnd 15: *1sc, sc2tog* (12)
Rnd 16: (sc2tog) 6x (6) **(fig. 23e)**

23e

• Finish stuffing head and finish piece off, leaving a long tail for sewing.

BODY: Gray yarn
• Make an adjustable ring.
Rnd 1: 6sc in ring (6)
Rnd 2: 2sc in each stitch (12)
Rnd 3: 1sc, 2sc in next st (18)
Rnd 4: *(1sc) 2x, 2sc in next st* (24)
Rnd 5: *(1sc) 3x, 2sc in next st* (30)
Rnds 6–9: 1sc in each st (30)
Rnd 10: *(1sc) 4x, 2sc in next st* (36)
Rnds 11–14: 1sc in each st (36)
Rnd 15: *(1sc) 4x, sc2tog* (30) **(fig. 23f)**

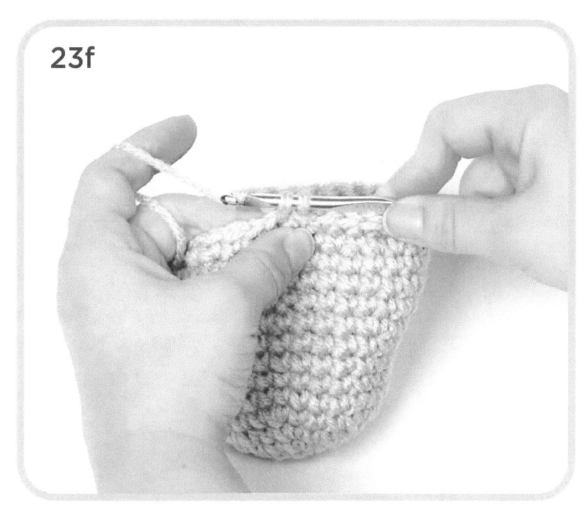

Rnd 16: *(1sc) 3x, sc2tog* (24)

• Stuff body firmly.

Rnd 17: *(1sc) 2x, sc2tog* (18)

Rnd 18: *1sc, sc2tog* (12)

Rnd 19: (sc2tog) 6x (6)

• Finish it off stuffing the body and finish off, leaving a long tail for sewing.

• Sew on the head, arms, legs, and tail.

mouse

FROM RACHELLE SMITH IN SALT LAKE CITY, UTAH

The early bird gets the worm, and this clever mouse has found the cheese! This little critter might be the quietest mouse you'll ever meet but he'll have your family and friends squeaking with delight!

what you'll need:

- worsted weight acrylic yarn in tan
- F/5 (3.75 mm) crochet hook

- size 10 crochet thread in yellow
- size 5 (1.70 mm) steel crochet hook
- black safety eyes (9 mm)
- pink safety nose (9 mm)
- chenille needle
- stuffing

FINISHED SIZE: About 6 inches tall

Instructions

- -

HEAD: Tan yarn
• Make an adjustable ring.
Rnd 1: 6sc into ring (6)
Rnd 2: 1sc in each stitch (6)
Rnd 3: *(1sc) 2x, 2sc in next stitch* (8)
Rnd 4: *1sc, 2sc in next stitch* (12)
Rnd 5: *(1sc) 2x, 2sc in next stitch* (16)
Rnd 6: *(1sc) 3x, 2sc in next stitch* (20)
Rnd 7: *(1sc) 4x, 2sc in next stitch* (24)
Rnd 8: 1sc in each stitch (24)
Rnd 9: *(1sc) 4x, sc2tog* (20)
Rnd 10: *(1sc) 3x, sc2tog* (16)
• Attach eyes and nose.
Rnd 11: *(1sc) 2x, sc2tog* (12)
• Stuff head.
Rnd 12: *1sc in next stitch, sc2tog* (8) **(fig. 24a)**

24a

Rnd 13: (sc2tog) 4x (4)

• Finish off, leaving a tail for sewing.

• Sew the head closed.

BODY: Tan yarn

• Make an adjustable ring.

Rnd 1: 8sc into ring

Rnd 2: 2sc in each stitch (16)

Rnd 3: *1sc in next stitch, 2sc in next stitch* (24)

Rnd 4: *(1sc) 2x, 2sc in next stitch* (32)

Rnds 5–7: 1sc in each stitch (32)

Rnd 8: *(1sc) 2x, sc2tog* (24)

Rnd 9: 1sc in each stitch (24)

Rnd 10: *1sc in next stitch, sc2tog* (16)

• Stuff the body.

Rnd 11: 1sc in each stitch (16)

Rnd 12: (sc2tog) 8x (8)

Rnd 13: 1sc in each stitch
- Finish off, leaving a tail for sewing.
- Stuff the neck and sew the head to the body. **(fig. 24b)**

24b

EAR (MAKE 2): Tan yarn

• Make an adjustable ring.

Rnd 1: 6sc into ring (6)

Rnd 2: 2sc in each stitch (12)

Rnd 3: *1sc in next stitch, 2sc in next stitch* (18)

• Finish off, leaving a tail, and sew to the head.

ARM (MAKE 2): Tan yarn

• Leave a long tail at the beginning to use later to sew the arm to the body.

• Ch 4 and sl st in first ch. **(fig. 24c)**

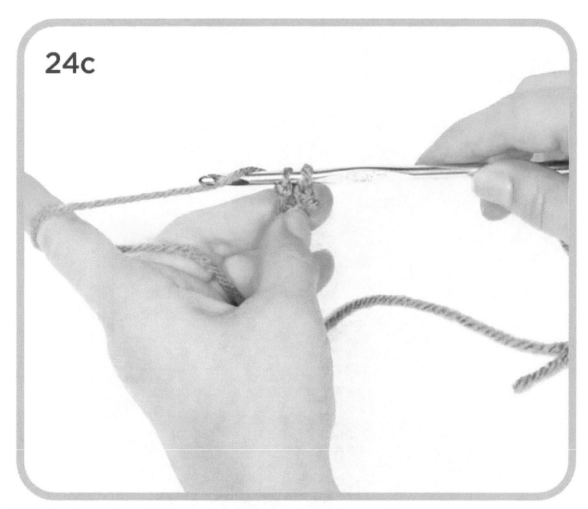

24c

Rnd 1: 4sc into ring (4)

Rnds 2–7: 1sc in each stitch (4)

Rows 8–10: turn, ch 1, 1sc in next 2 stitches (2) **(fig. 24d)**

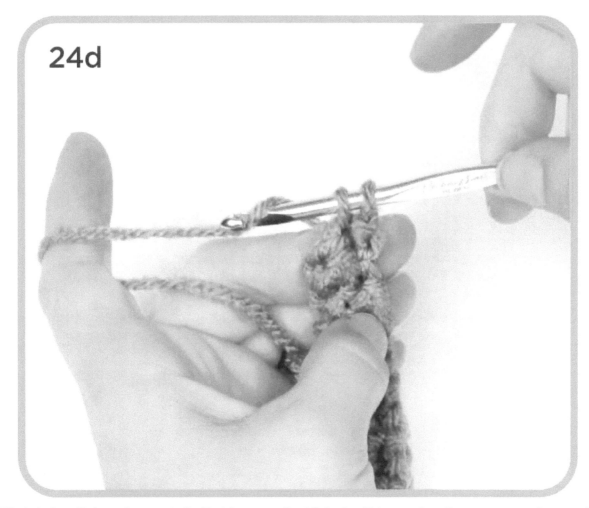

24d

- Finish it off, leaving a tail. Fold rows 8–10 in half to make the paw, and sew this shut, stuffing just a little before closing it.

FOOT (MAKE 2): Tan yarn
Row 1: ch 9, 1sc in 2nd ch from hook and across (8)
Rows 2–6: turn, ch 1, 1sc in each stitch (8)
- Finish it off, leaving a tail for sewing.
- Fold it in half and sew it along the edges, lightly stuffing the toe area before closing up. Don't stuff it too much, or the back end of the foot won't lay flat under the body. **(fig. 24e)**

24e

TAIL: Tan yarn
- Ch 30, finish it off, leaving a tail. Sew one end into the tail and the other end into the body, joining the tail securely to the body as you do so.

CHEESE:
- Switch to the steel hook and crochet thread.

SIDES & BACK: Yellow thread
Row 1: ch 9, 1sc in 2nd ch from hook and across (8)
Rows 2–18: turn, ch 1, 1sc in each stitch (8)
Row 19: turn, ch 1, 1sc across through back loops only (8) **(fig. 24f)**

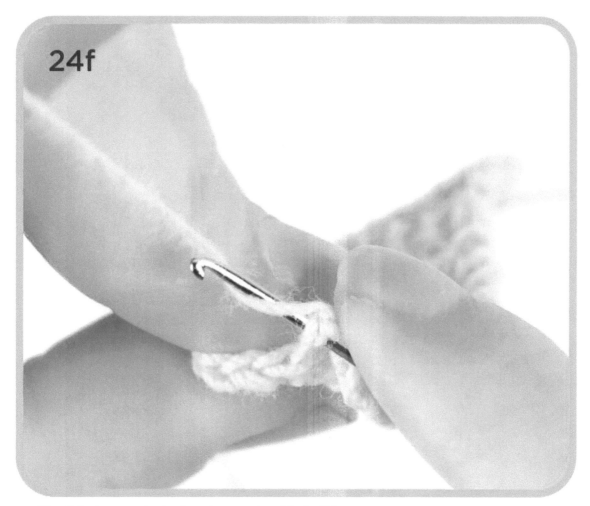

Rows 20–22: turn, ch 1, 1sc in each stitch (8)

• Finish it off, leaving a tail. Sew the last row to the first row. You have created the sides and the back of the cheese.

TOP & BOTTOM (MAKE 2):

Row 1: ch 6, 1sc in 2nd ch from hook and across (5) **(fig. 24g)**

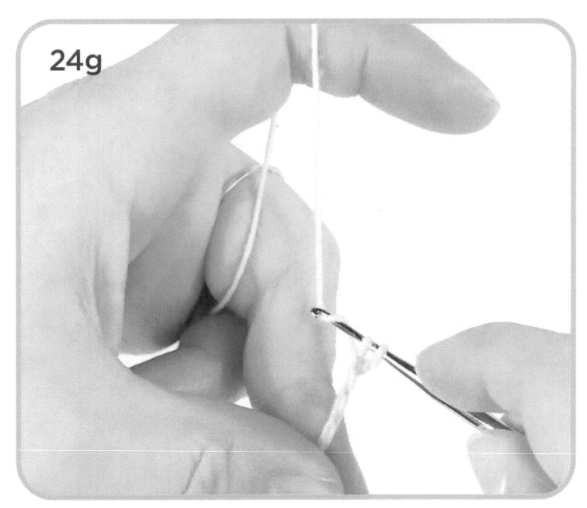

Row 2: turn, ch 1, 1sc in next stitch, sc2tog, 2sc (4)

Row 3: turn, ch 1, 1sc in next stitch, sc2tog, 1sc (3)

Row 4: turn, ch 1, 1sc in next stitch, sc2tog (2)

Row 5: turn, ch 1, sc2tog (1)

Row 6: turn, ch 1, 1sc (1)

• Fasten off, leaving a long tail. Sew to the top and bottom of the cheese, stuffing lightly before you close up. Use the loose ends to sew the cheese to the mouse's hands—be sure to sew it tightly, or his arms may start pulling the stitches apart. **(fig. 24h)**

24h

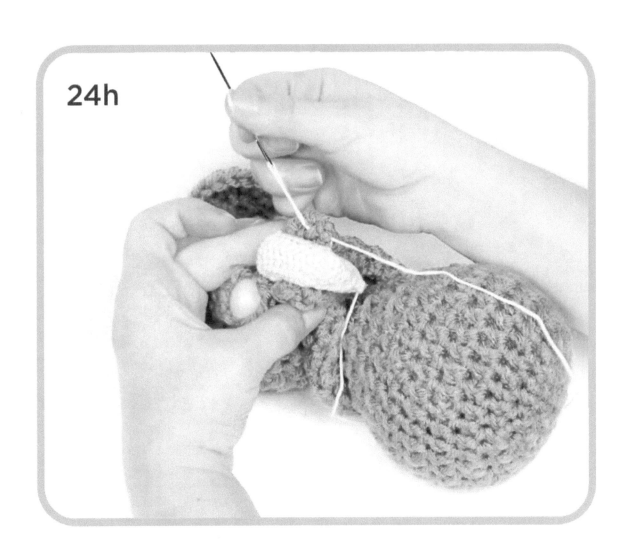

skunk

FROM DENISE FERGUSON IN PENNSYLVANIA

These stinky little creatures are usually to be avoided, but let me introduce you to the best skunk in town. Not only does this guy not smell, but his claws are soft so he won't try to den up in the corner of your couch. Make a whole family of skunks to love and share!

what you'll need:

- **G/6 (4.0 mm) crochet hook**
- **worsted weight acrylic yarn in white, black and pink**
- **black safety eyes (9 mm)**

FINISHED SIZE: About 6 inches long

Instructions

LEGS (MAKE 4): Black yarn
• Make an adjustable ring.
Rnd 1: 6sc in ring (6)
Rnd 2-4: 1sc in each st (6)
• Finish off, leaving a long tail for sewing.

EARS (MAKE 2): Black yarn
• Make an adjustable ring.
Rnd 1: 3sc in ring (3)
• Finish off, leaving a long tail.

BODY: Black yarn
• Make an adjustable ring.
Rnd 1: 6sc in ring (6)
Rnd 2: 1sc in each st (6)
Rnd 3: *1sc, 2sc in next st* (9) **(fig. 25a)**

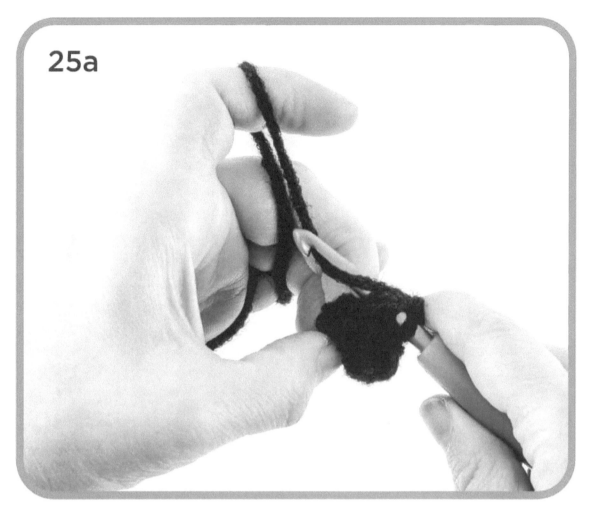

Rnd 4–5: 1sc in each st (9)

Rnd 6: 2sc in each st (18)

Rnd 7–8: 1sc in each st (18)

- Stitch on the nose with pink yarn, attach safety eyes between rounds 5 and 6, sew on the ears between rounds 7 and 8, and stitch on eyelashes with white yarn. **(fig. 25b)**

25b

Rnd 9: *1sc, sc2tog* (12)
Rnd 10: *1sc, 2sc in next st* (18)
Rnd 11: *2sc, 2sc in next st* (24)
Rnd 12–21: 1sc in each st (24)
Rnd 22: *2sc, sc2tog* (18)
Rnd 23: *1sc, sc2tog* (12)
Rnd 24: sc2tog around (6) **(fig. 25c)**

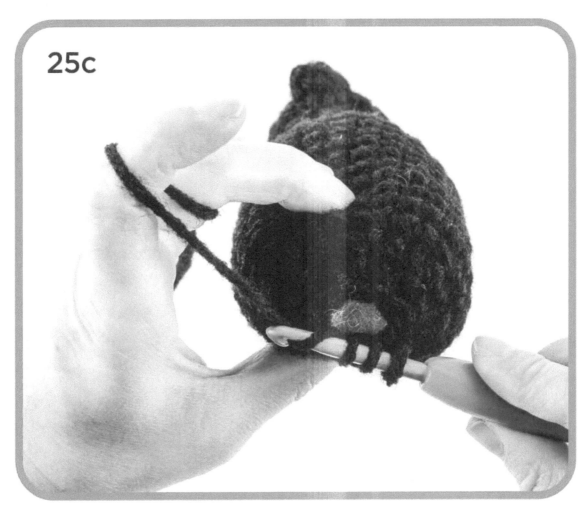

25c

• Finish off and weave in the ends.

BODY STRIPE: Start with white yarn
• Ch 2, start in 2nd ch from hook. Work back and forth in rows, turning work.
Row 1: 1sc, ch 1, turn (1)
Row 2: 1sc, ch 1, turn (1)
Row 3: 2sc in each st, ch 1, turn (2)
Row 4: 2sc in each st, ch 1, turn (4) **(fig. 25d)**

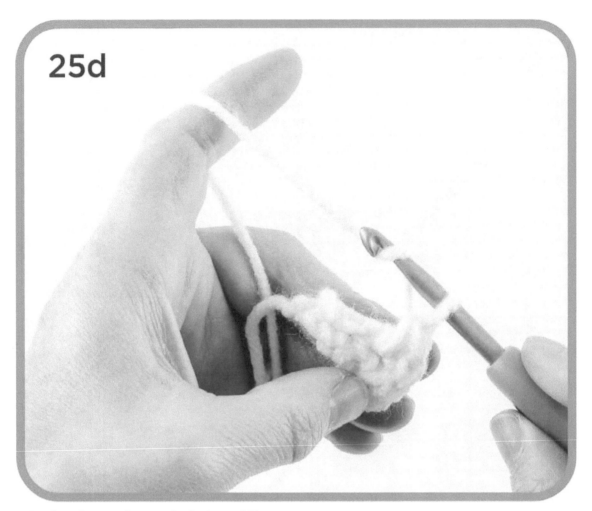

Row 5: 1sc in each st, ch 1, turn (4)

Row 6: 2sc in first st, 2sc, 2sc in next st, ch 1, turn (6)

Row 7–21: 1sc in each st, ch 1, turn (6)

• Finish off.

• Starting at row 1, pull a loop of black yarn with your hook from the underside to the topside in the spaces between rows. Repeat to draw another loop into and through the first. Repeat until you reach the end of the stripe, finish off and sew stripe onto the body. **(fig. 25e)**

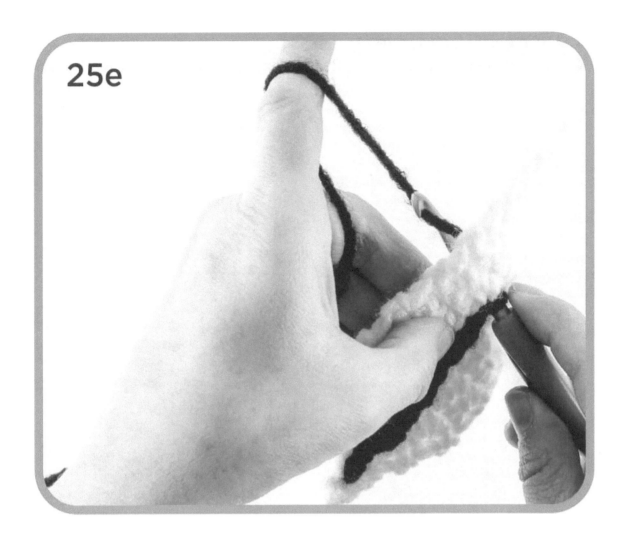

25e

TAIL: yarn
• Make an adjustable ring.
Rnd 1: 6sc in ring (6)
Rnd 2: 1sc in each st (6)
Rnd 3: *2sc, 2sc in next st* (8)
Rnd 4: *1sc, 2sc in next st* (12)
Rnd 5: 1sc in each st (12)
Rnd 6: *1sc, 2sc in next st* (18)
Rnd 7–15: 1sc in each st (18)
Rnd 16: *1sc, sc2tog* (12)
• Finish off, leaving a long tail for sewing.

TAIL STRIPE: Start with white yarn
• Ch 2, start in 2nd ch from hook.
Row 1: 1sc, ch 1, turn (1)
Row 2: 2sc in each st, ch 1, turn (2)

Row 3: 2sc in each st, ch 1, turn (4)
Row 4: 2sc in first st, sc in next 2 st, 2sc in next st, ch 1, turn (6) **(see fig. 25f)**

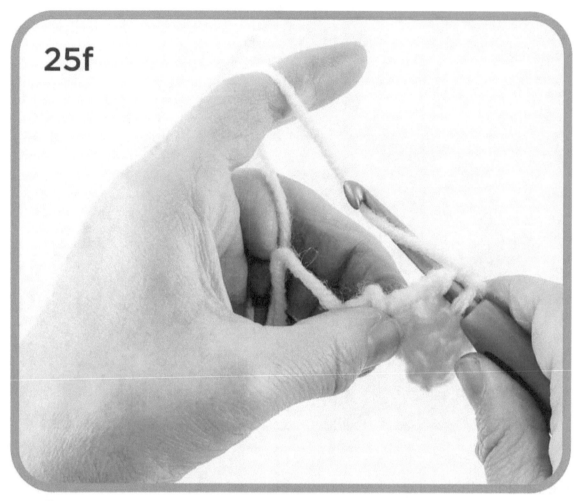

25f

Row 5–16: 1sc in each st, ch 1, turn (6)
• Finish off.
• Finish off, and sew the stripe onto the tail.

FINISHING:
  1. Sew the tail onto the end of the body, matching up the stripe. **(fig. 25g)**

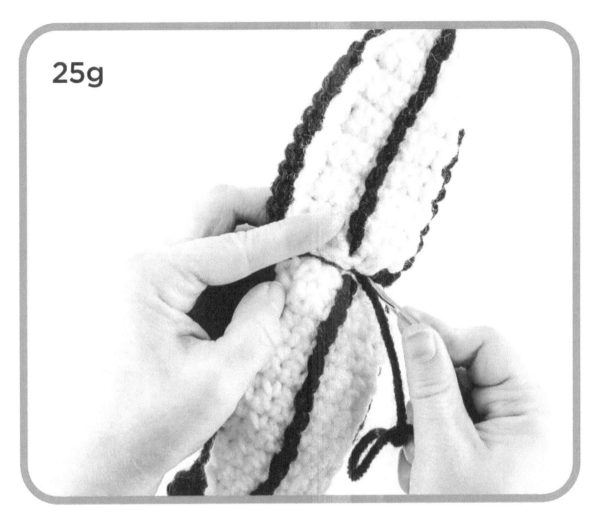

2. Sew all four legs onto the underside of the body. Weave in the ends.

tortoise

FROM DENISE FERGUSON IN PENNSYLVANIA

This tortoise will live for years, just like his wild counterpart. But this guy has a soft shell, improving his snuggle capabilities. And unlike his wild counterpart, he is very social and enjoys the company of family and friends.

what you'll need:

- **worsted weight yarn in green and bright green**
- **G/6 (4.0 mm) crochet hook**
- **black safety eyes (9 mm)**
- **chenille needle**
- **stuffing**

FINISHED SIZE: About 7 inches long

Instructions

SHELL SPOTS (MAKE 7): Green yarn
• Make an adjustable ring.
Rnd 1: 6sc in ring (6)
Rnd 2: 2sc in each st (12)
Rnd 3: *1sc, 2sc in next st* (18) **(fig. 26a)**

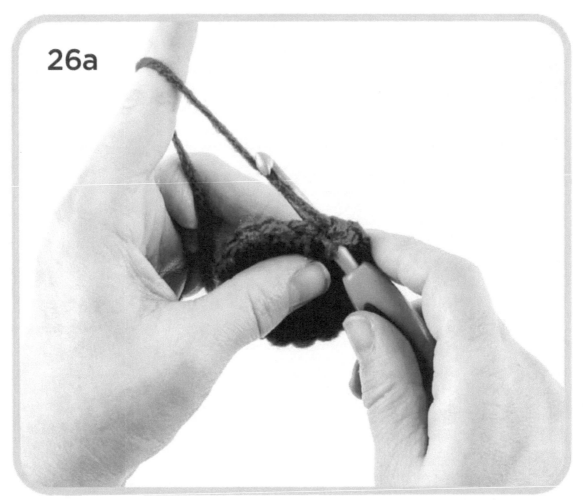

• Finish it off, leaving a long tail to sew onto the shell.

SHELL TOP: Bright green yarn
• ch 6, start in 2nd ch from hook.
Rnd 1: 1sc, 4sc, 3sc in next ch, 3sc, 2sc in next ch (12) **(fig. 26b)**

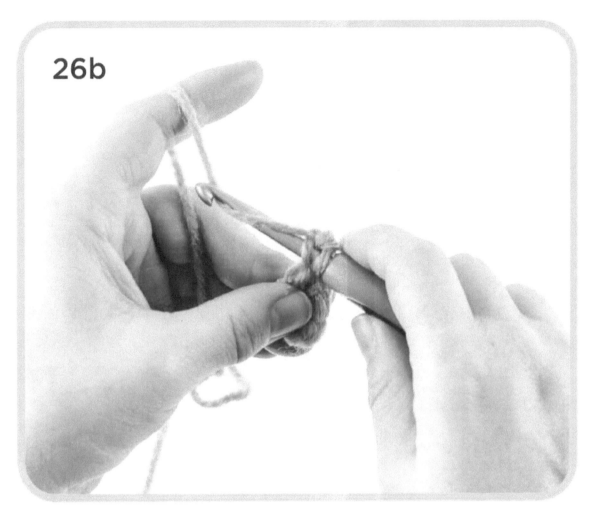

26b

Rnd 2: *1sc, 2sc in next st* (18)
Rnd 3: *2sc, 2sc in next st* (24)
Rnd 4: *3sc, 2sc in next st* (30)
Rnd 5: *4sc, 2sc in next st* (36)
Rnd 6: *5sc, 2sc in next st* (42)
Rnd 7: *6sc, 2sc in next st* (48)
Rnd 8: *7sc, 2sc in next st* (54)
Rnd 9–12: 1sc in each st (54)
Rnd 13: hdc in front loop only of each st (54) **(fig. 26c)**

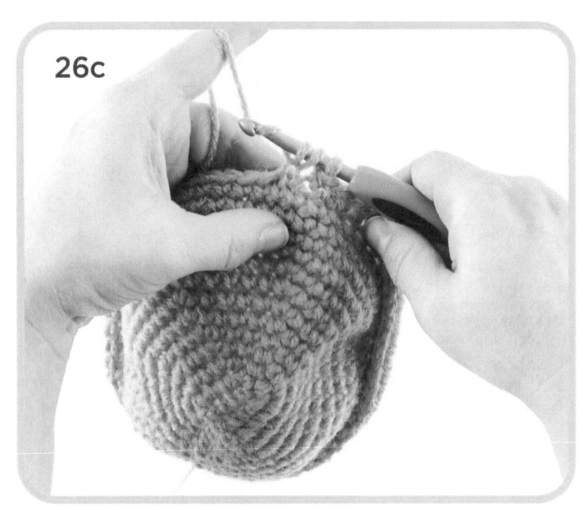

26c

• Finish off and weave in the ends.

SHELL BOTTOM: Bright green yarn

• Ch 6, start in 2nd ch from hook.

Rnd 1: 1sc, 3sc, 3sc in next ch, 3sc, 2sc in next ch (12)

Rnd 2: *1sc, 2sc in next st* (18)

Rnd 3: *2sc, 2sc in next st* (24)

Rnd 4: *3sc, 2sc in next st* (30)

Rnd 5: *4sc, 2sc in next st* (36) **(fig. 26d)**

26d

Rnd 6: *5sc, 2sc in next st* (42)
Rnd 7: *6sc, 2sc in next st* (48)
Rnd 8: *7sc, 2sc in next st* (54)
• Finish off, leaving a long tail to sew onto the shell top.

LEGS (MAKE 4): Bright green yarn
• Make an adjustable ring.
Rnd 1: 6sc in ring (6)
Rnd 2: 2sc in each st (12)
Rnd 3–9: 1sc in each st (12)
• Finish off, leaving a long tail to sew onto the shell.

HEAD: Bright green yarn
• Make an adjustable ring.
Rnd 1: 6sc in ring (6)
Rnd 2: 2sc in each st (12)
Rnd 3: *1sc, 2sc in next st* (18)

Rnd 4–7: 1sc in each st (18)
• Attach safety eyes between rounds 4 and 5. **(fig. 26e)**

Rnd 8: *1sc, sc2tog* (12)
Rnd 9–12: 1sc in each st (12)
• Finish off, leaving a long tail to sew onto the shell.

FINISHING:
1. Sew spots onto shell top. **(fig. 26f)**

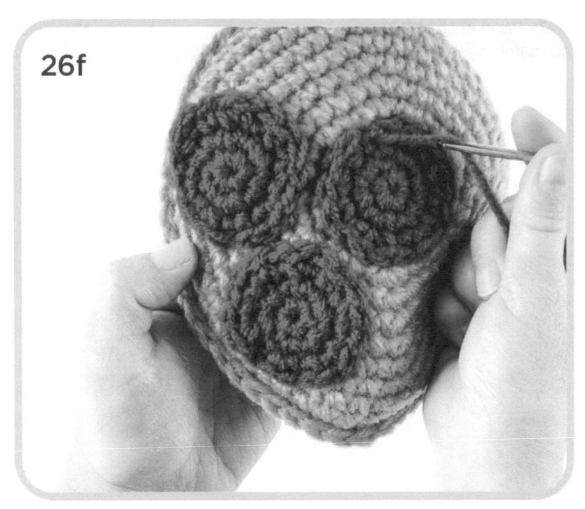

26f

2. Partially stitch the shell bottom to the top, stitching through the front loops from round 13 of the shell top. Stuff the shell, finish stitching around, and weave in the ends. **(fig. 26g)**

26g

3. Sew the head and legs to the bottom of the shell, and weave in the ends.

Where to Find the Artists

Aeron Aanstoos's main focus is sea creatures, all of which are magical in their own way. See them all at www.edafedd.com.

Pauline Abayon learned to crochet from her mother. Her favorite things to make are dolls, hats, and doilies. She sells a lot of her work on Etsy.com: www.stripeyblue.etsy.com.

M. Bridges works every day in her studio creating adorable little amigurumi creations for her business. To find all her adorable creations, visit her online at moonscreations.com.

Teri Crews spends a lot of her time crocheting, knitting, and caring for her family and two dogs. You can find her crochet animals and dolls at tcrewsdesigns.com.

Sanda Jelic Dobrosavljev started making amigurumi after her daughter was born. She now sells her fanciful patterns as well as one-of-a-kind dolls on her website pepika.com.

Denise Ferguson is the one-woman show behind Yummy Pancake, where she sells delicious-looking amigurumi plushies and patterns. You can find all her creations at yummypancake.com.

Karla Fitch was inspired to make amigurumi while listening to her daughter's nursery music, hence the name The Itsy Bitsy Spider. You can find all her amigurumi gifts and patterns at theitsybitsyspider.etsy.com.

Amy Gaines works on patterns in-between moments of parenting her daughter. She has tons of cute designs and kits available at amygaines.etsy.com.

Kandice Soraya Grote's business name Spud's Stitches came from her dad, who nicknamed her Spud because she looked like a little potato.

Katja Heinlein put her hooks away for a long time, but always missed art and design. She decided to give it a try again and now makes amigurumi designs from her home in Germany. Check out her stuff at np-trade.de.

Heather Jarmusz is an artist from Illinois. You can find her work at hamandeggs.etsy.com.

Alicia Kachmar is a sometimes teacher, freelance writer, nurse, and nursing PhD student, in addition to making adorable amigurumi. Find her at aliciakachmar.com.

Madelyn spends her days sipping chai tea, playing with her dogs, and making sweet amigurumi plushies and patterns.

Brigitte Read lives in Glasgow, Scotland. She admits to having a crush on classical Rome because the oldest existing piece of crochet is a Roman sock, which inspired the name of her blog, littlegreen.typepad.com/romansock.

Victoria Rodriguez loves crocheting, blogging, and drawing.

Amanda C. Scofield has three kids, so she doesn't have much time for crochet. But when she does, she makes it incredibly cute amigurumi.

Rachelle Smith sells a plethora of adorable patterns as well as ready-made crochet friends at yayhookdcrochet.etsy.com.

Sweees learned to crochet after a coworker taught her the basics, and now she shares the results with you!

Celia Tseng learned to crochet from her mother. She lives in Baldwinsville, NY, where she works as a systems engineer.

Amanda Lynn Wilhite sells everything from crochet accessories to toys in her online shop indigocrochet.etsy.com.

Appendix: Pattern Templates

The templates shown here are available for download and printing here.

PROJECT 4: Chick - Beak

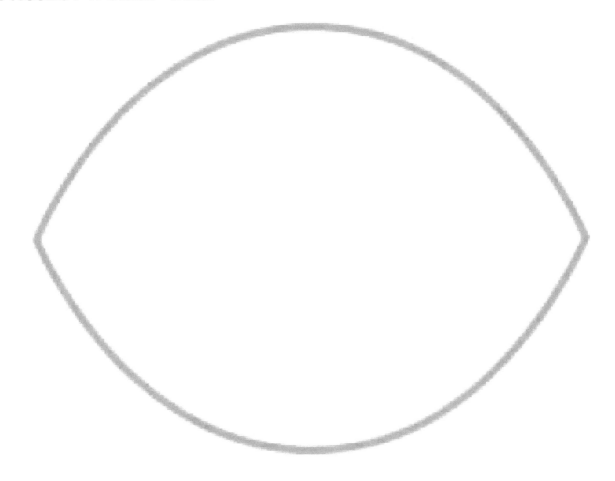

PROJECT 7: Koala - Nose

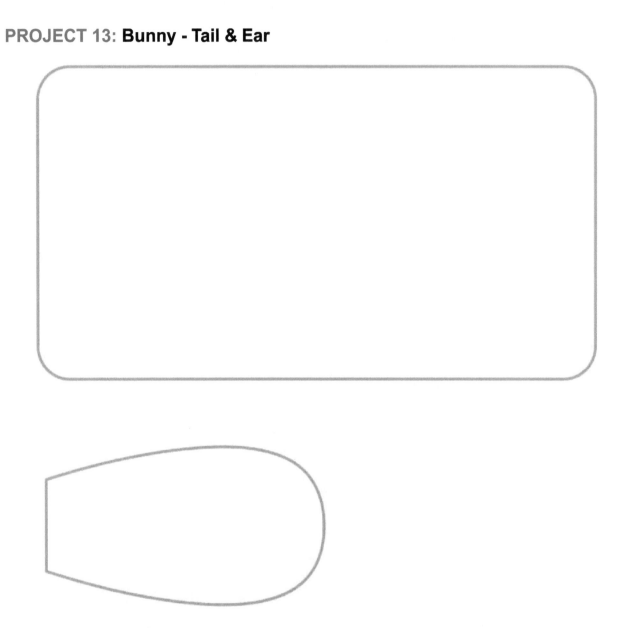

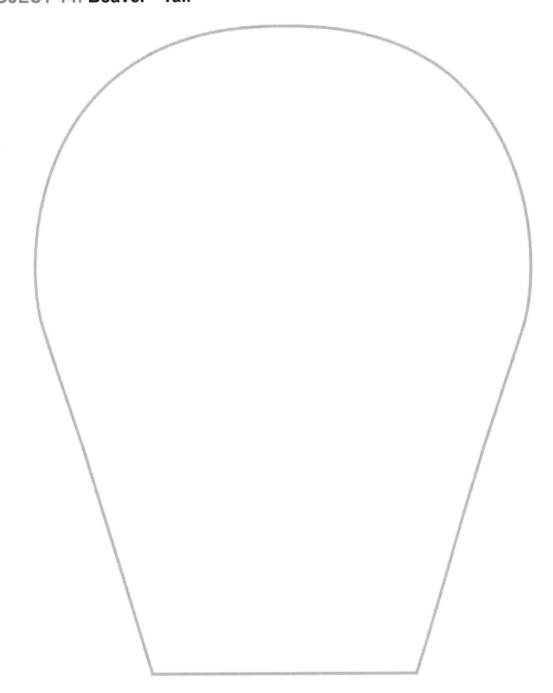

PROJECT 20: Raccoon - Eyes

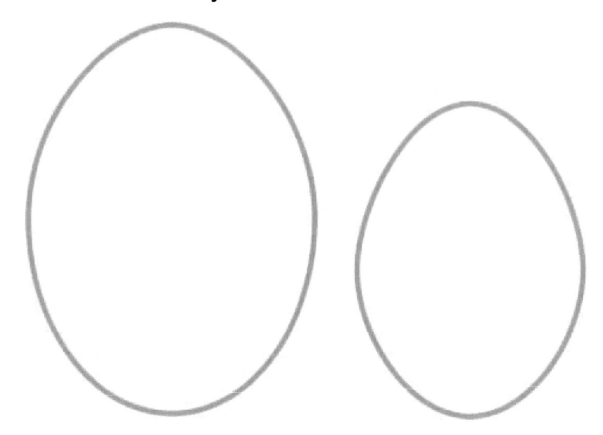

25699435R00173